W9-ARJ-736

Exploring **C**anada

YUKON TERRITORY

Titles in the Exploring Canada series include:

Alberta

British Columbia

Manitoba

Ontario

Quebec

Exploring Canada

YUKON TERRITORY

by Steven Ferry, Blake Harris,
and Liz Szynkowski

LUCENT
BOOKS®

THOMSON
★
GALE

SOUTH HUNTINGTON
PUBLIC LIBRARY
HUNTINGTON STATION, NY 11746

San Diego • Detroit • New York • San Francisco • Cleveland • New Haven, Conn. • Waterville, Maine • London • Munich

917.19
Ferry

THOMSON

GALE

Development, management, design, and composition by Pre-Press Company, Inc.

© 2003 by Lucent Books. Lucent Books is an imprint of The Gale Group, Inc.,
a division of Thomson Learning, Inc.

Lucent Books® and Thomson Learning™ are trademarks used herein under license.

For more information, contact
Lucent Books
27500 Drake Rd.
Farmington Hills, MI 48331-3535
Or you can visit our Internet site at http://www.gale.com

ALL RIGHTS RESERVED.
No part of this work covered by the copyright hereon may be reproduced or used in any form or by
any means—graphic, electronic, or mechanical, including photocopying, recording, taping, Web dis-
tribution or information storage retrieval systems—without the written permission of the publisher.

LIBRARY OF CONGRESS CATALOGING-IN-PUBLICATION DATA

Ferry, Steven, 1953–
    Yukon Territory / by Steven Ferry.
        p. cm. — (Exploring Canada series)
Summary: Examines the history, geography, climate, industries, people,
and culture of Canada's most remote and untamed region.
Includes bibliographical references and index.
    ISBN 1-59018-053-4 (hardback : alk. paper).
    1. Yukon Territory—Juvenile literature. 2. Yukon
Territory—History—Juvenile literature. [1. Yukon Territory.
2. Canada.]   I. Title.   II. Series.
    F1091.4 .F47 2003
    971.91—dc21
                                                                2002004110

Printed in the United States of America

30652001269572

Contents

Foreword

Any truly accurate portrait of Canada would have to be painted in sharp contrasts, for this is a long-inhabited but only recently settled land. It is a vast and expansive region peopled by a predominantly urban population. Canada is also a nation of natives and immigrants that, as its Prime Minister Lester Pearson remarked in the late 1960s, has "not yet found a Canadian soul except in time of war." Perhaps it is in these very contrasts that this elusive national identity is waiting to be found.

Canada as an inhabited place is among the oldest in the Western Hemisphere, having accepted prehistoric migrants more than eleven thousand years ago after they crossed a land bridge where the Bering Strait now separates Alaska from Siberia. Canada is also the site of the New World's earliest European settlement, L'Anse aux Meadows on the northern tip of Newfoundland Island. A band of Vikings lived there briefly some five hundred years before Columbus reached the West Indies in 1492.

Yet as a nation Canada is still a relative youngster on the world scene. It gained its independence almost a century after the American Revolution and half a century after the wave of nationalist uprisings in South America. Canada did not include Newfoundland until 1949 and could not amend its own constitution without approval from the British Parliament until 1982. "The Sleeping Giant," as Canada is sometimes known, came within a whisker of losing a province in 1995, when the people of Quebec narrowly voted down an independence referendum.

In 1999 Canada carved out a new territory, Nunavut, which has a population equal to that of Key West, Florida, spread over an area the size of Alaska and California combined.

As the second largest country in the world (after Russia), the land itself is also famously diverse. British Columbia's "Pocket Desert" near the town of Osoyoos is the northernmost desert in North America. A few hundred miles away, in Alberta's Banff National Park, one can walk on the Columbia Icefields, the largest nonpolar icecap in the world. In parts of Manitoba and the Yukon glacially created sand dunes creep slowly across the landscape. Quebec and Ontario have so many lakes in the boundless north that tens of thousands remain unnamed.

One can only marvel at a place where the contrasts range from the profound (the first medical use of insulin) to the mundane (the invention of Trivial Pursuit); the sublime (the poetry of Ontario-born Robertson Davies) to the ridiculous (the comic antics of Ontario-born Jim Carrey); the British (ever-so-quaint Victoria) to the French (Montreal, the world's second-largest French-speaking city); and the environmental (Greenpeace was founded in Vancouver) to the industrial (refuse from nickel mining near Sudbury, Ontario left a landscape so barren that American astronauts used it to train for their moon walks).

Given these contrasts and conflicts, can this national experiment known as Canada survive? Or to put it another way, what is it that unites as Canadians the elderly Inuit woman selling native crafts in the Yukon; the millionaire businessman-turned-restaurateur recently emigrated from Hong Kong to Vancouver; the mixed-French (Métis) teenager living in a rural settlement in Manitoba; the cosmopolitan French-speaking professor of archeology in Quebec City; and the raw-boned Nova Scotia fisherman struggling to make a living? These are questions only Canadians can answer, and perhaps will have to face for many decades.

A true portrait of Canada can't, therefore, be provided by a brief essay, any more than a snapshot captures the entire life of a centenarian. But the Exploring Canada Series can offer an illuminating overview of individual provinces and territories. Each book smartly summarizes an area's geography, history, arts and culture, daily life, and contemporary issues. Read individually or as a series, they show that what Canadians undeniably have in common is a shared heritage as people who came, whether in past millennia or last year, to a land with a difficult climate and a challenging geography, yet somehow survived and worked with one another to form a vibrant whole.

The Spell of the Yukon

The Yukon is a rugged, untamed land that has much to teach if people are willing to learn. Its lessons certainly are a colorful part of North America's heritage. Its history is full of intriguing and sometimes dubious characters who faced boundless perils and adventures. Even today, many thousands of people go to the Yukon each year just to touch and relive some of that past.

Yet the Yukon has deeper values to teach, not just about yesterday, but also about who we are and what we can strive to achieve—even in the most adverse environmental conditions. Martha Louise Black, a Kansas native who hiked over the difficult Chilkoot Pass into the Yukon while pregnant in 1898 after her first husband abandoned her along the way, wrote about the change she experienced as a result of coming to settle in this difficult land:

> I became eager to live, to accomplish something worthwhile, something of which my three boys would be proud. This is still the dominant motive in my life. I could not shake off the lure of the Klondike. My thoughts were continually of that vast new rugged country, its stark and splendid mountains, its lordly Yukon River, with its streams and its deep blue lakes, its midnight sun, its gold and green of summer, its never-ending dark of winter, illuminated by golden stars and flaming northern lights. What I wanted was not shelter and safety, but liberty and opportunity.[1]

Such is the power of the Yukon. Its challenges often seem to bring out the best in people. And its communities continue

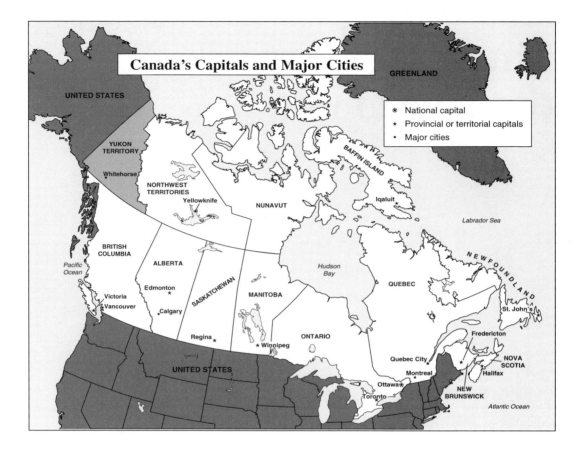

Canada's Capitals and Major Cities

- ⊛ National capital
- ★ Provincial or territorial capitals
- · Major cities

■ *Hikers pause to appreciate the rugged beauty of Mount Logan in the Yukon's Kluane National Park.*

deep social traditions of cooperation, where it is not just one's own survival that is important. The survival and well-being of one's neighbors are important as well, for ultimately what we make of this earth, we make together.

The Yukoners believe that the Yukon is like no other place on earth. And in many ways, they may be right. As the famous Yukon poet Robert Service wrote in "The Spell of the Yukon":

There's a land where the mountains are nameless,
And the rivers all run God knows where;
There are lives that are erring and aimless,
And deaths that just hang by a hair;
There are hardships that nobody reckons;
There are valleys unpeopled and still;
There's a land—oh, it beckons and beckons,
And I want to go back—and I will.

Land of Challenge

T he Yukon Territory, situated in the extreme north-western part of Canada, is the ninth largest of the thirteen Canadian provinces and territories, representing approximately 5 percent of the country's landmass. Yet the Yukon, as it is often abbreviated, covers an immense area. Its roughly 186,000 square miles (483,000 square kilometers) make it larger than any of the American states with the exception of Alaska and Texas, and approximately three times the size of New England.

The Yukon lies north of the province of British Columbia and east of the state of Alaska. The Yukon is a wild land of mineral wealth and scenic diversity that even today remains sparsely settled. Of all the regions of Canada, this part was the last to be explored, largely because travel was so difficult. During summer months, swampy, mosquito-infested terrain prevented most travel by land. Winters brought deep snow and extreme cold that froze the rivers—the first routes into the region. Settlers soon discovered that the environment was brutal for those lacking wilderness survival skills.

A True Frontier

Over the years, the Yukon has been called "the last great wilderness of North America," the "land of the midnight sun," and perhaps most romantically "the last frontier." In the late 1800s, former Canadian prime minister Sir Wilfrid Laurier

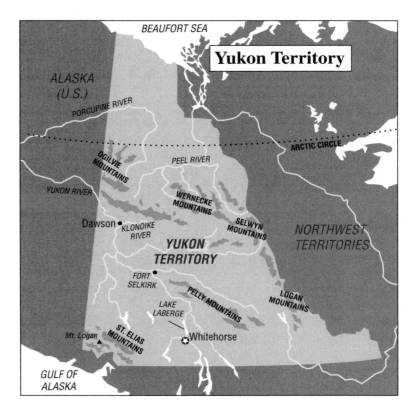

said of the region, "Here indeed is a true frontier and one that will never be fully conquered."[2]

The people who live in the Yukon today would agree. The challenge of the land has molded a distinct Yukon personality or character. As one Yukoner described it, "It may be the harshness, at times, or the length of the winters or any number of indeterminate factors that make Yukoners different, a difference so appreciated by other Yukoners."[3] Sharing nature's adversities, especially the long, dark winters, fosters a camaraderie and a community spirit that gives residents a special appreciation of each other and the land they call home.

The harsh environment, no doubt, is one reason the Yukon is so sparsely populated. The Yukon's total population in Canada's 2001 census was a little shy of twenty-nine thousand, about the same as the population of the third-largest city (Laramie) in the least populated American state (Wyoming, which is about half of Yukon's size but has more than fifteen times Yukon's population). The Yukon's population includes approximately six thousand native, or "First Nations," people. The capital city of Whitehorse, the largest municipality in the territory, harbors some 70 percent of the entire Yukon population. The next two largest towns, Dawson City (frequently referred to simply as Dawson) and Watson Lake, house approximately two thousand residents each. That leaves about five thousand people scattered in towns and villages throughout the vast Yukon Territory.

Much of the Yukon's total area is still a unique wilderness that has remained untouched by roads. This land is rich in forests, rivers, lakes, valleys, and abundant species of wildlife. But the most prominent topographical characteristic is undoubtedly the rugged mountain ranges that stretch across much of the region. In fact, this was the first land feature to be seen by explorers.

Prominent Mountain Ranges

In 1741, as the Danish-Russian explorer Vitus Bering was sailing through the Gulf of Alaska, he saw a massive mountain looming over the horizon of the Alaskan coastline. This cloud-swept peak was the first feature of the future Yukon Territory to be sighted by a nonnative. As this occurred on July 16, which was celebrated in Europe as St. Elias Day, Bering named the mountain Mount St. Elias. Bering died on that journey, but his men sailed back to Siberia, bringing with them stories of an inland mountain so high that it was seen from a distance towering above all else. In fact, Mount St. Elias is the second-highest mountain in Canada, after the Yukon's Mount Logan in the same range. Later, that entire range became known as the St. Elias Mountains.

The St. Elias mountain range has the world's second-largest permanent ice fields, off of which creep glaciers that are thousands of feet thick. One of these glaciers was so massive that when it broke off in 1850, it blocked the entire width of the Alsek River, causing a huge lake to form. When this ice dam broke suddenly, it took two days for the rushing waters to empty out.

Inland from the huge coastal mountains are numerous smaller mountain ranges including another heavily glaciated mountain range called the Selwyn Mountains, along the Yukon's border with the Northwest Territories. Elevations in the Selwyns range up to 9,750 feet (2,972 meters). In the Yukon's west, along the border with Alaska, the Ogilvie Mountains are considered extremely rugged due to their high peaks and deep valleys. Because of these treacherous conditions, both the Selwyns and the Ogilvies remained virtually unexplored until after World War II. Even today only about fifty people live in these mountains.

The mountain ranges so prevalent throughout the Yukon create a breathtaking landscape. Author Martha Louise Black, who left Chicago as a young woman to spend the rest of her life in the Yukon, wrote, "The campsite commanded a magnificent view of snow-capped peaks, ranged round in fanlike folds."[4] In addition to affording a spectacular view, the Yukon's mountains influence the weather conditions more than any other factor in the region.

■ Climbing Mount Logan

Mount Logan is composed of granite and is among the most massive mountains in the world. It is also Canada's highest mountain, towering at 19,551 feet (5,959 meters) above sea level. In 1925, a team of Canadian and American climbers set out on a sixty-five-day expedition to climb the mountain. Only two members of the team managed to reach the top. Since then, thirteen different routes have been taken in attempts to reach the summit. With its 10,000-foot rock faces, many deep crevasses, and frequent avalanches it is still considered to be among the most ambitious and demanding climbs in North America. Guided ascents often take three weeks, not including the time it takes to trek to the base of the mountain across 60 miles (100 kilometers) of glacier. And do not count on getting rescued if things go wrong—it is so remote that it is difficult to arrange for emergency aircraft and rescuers may face delays due to weather conditions.

■ *A climber stands atop the snow-covered peak of Mount Logan, Canada's highest mountain.*

A Challenging Climate

The Selwyn and the Ogilvie Mountains together act as a wind barrier, shunting aside arctic air masses descending from the north. The coastal mountain ranges also increase rainfall on the west-facing slopes, since precipitation condenses as clouds gain elevation and cool. The effect is to shelter the Yukon's interior from the moisture of the Pacific Ocean, causing the climate to be quite dry. In the fall, Yukon valleys experience storms and frequent periods of heavy fog, but through all other seasons, the weather remains fairly dry. The annual precipitation levels range between about 8 inches (20 centimeters) in the north and 28 inches (70 centimeters) in the south.

Winter brings bone-chilling temperatures but, in many places, relatively little snowfall. The Yukon's annual snowfall of between 25 and 100 inches (60 and 250 centimeters) is much less than is experienced in the neighboring Northwest Territories or Alaska.

Another unusual feature of Yukon's winters is a strange reversal of temperature patterns. Usually, as elevation increases, the temperature decreases. But in the Yukon, there are times when the valley temperatures reach −49°F (−45°C) whereas 3,000 feet (1,000 meters) higher up it may be 5°F (−15°C). This phenomenon is due to an inversion layer,

■ *The Nahanni River and Bologna Ridge in the Selwyn Mountains. The Yukon's mountains directly affect the region's weather conditions.*

common in parts of the Yukon from late October to early March, caused by a lack of wind and a settling of cold, moist, heavy air into the valleys.

The Yukon's lowest recorded temperature was −81°F (−63°C) on February 3, 1947, in Snag in southwest Yukon Territory. To this day it remains the coldest temperature ever recorded in North America. The average winter temperature is usually not as cold, but fluctuates between −4° to −22°F (−20° to −30°C). Melody Webb, who lived in the Yukon writes, "Winter's extreme cold changes the properties of the commonest materials of everyday life. Even the thickest metal grows brittle and breaks easily. Bare flesh that touches cold metal burns, and the slightest dampness from perspiration glues it to the metal. Cold this severe will transform a cup of hot coffee thrown into the air into a cloud of black steam, with nary a drop falling to the ground."[5]

Even spring and summer tend to be cool. Temperatures during June, July, and August average about 50° F (10°C) throughout the territory except in the extreme north, where it is colder. Despite these cool temperatures, summer marks the Yukon's growing season as the vegetation takes advantage of the long daylight hours. Along the Arctic coast, the sun does not set from May 19 to July 26. Farther south, the city of Whitehorse and towns like Watson Lake experience nineteen hours of sunshine each day. Dawson, which is farther to the north, has almost twenty-one hours of daylight. These prolonged periods of sunlight promote rapid growth in plants, which enables Yukoners to successfully grow some grain and vegetable crops. Wildflowers grow profusely during this period as well.

From Tundra to Desert

More than thirteen hundred plant species are found in the Yukon. A great number of common wildflowers such as fireweed, mountain poppies, and several types of wild orchids flourish in the area and can create a spectacular landscape. Martha Louise Black wrote, "For the first time in my life I saw hillsides of wild blue iris and lupine, or blue bonnet."[6]

The northernmost section of the Yukon is unforested tundra, characterized by subsoil that is always frozen (permafrost) and a very short growing season. These conditions allow only limited, low-growing vegetation to develop. Common tundra plants include lichens, mosses, and mounds of sedge grasses.

■ *Fireweed (left) thrives in the sunny Burwash Uplands in southwestern Yukon. Fireweed (below, detail) is one of 1,300 plant species found in the territory.*

The Yukon has an unusual area in its south, on the border with British Columbia, that is almost as barren. This is the Carcross Dunes, site of some of the tallest sand dunes in North America. Affectionately promoted as "the world's smallest desert," it covers only 1 square mile (2.6 square kilometers). The area gets too much precipitation to meet the strictest definition of a desert, and is more technically a "northern dune area" similar to a few others in Alaska and elsewhere. Geologists are not sure exactly how the Carcross Dunes were formed. The most prominent theory is that the sand accumulated from deposits at the bottom of large glacial

■ The Famous Lake Laberge

Poet Robert Service wrote a book of Yukon poems entitled *The Spell of the Yukon*. One of these poems, "The Cremation of Sam McGee," made Lake Laberge famous throughout the English-speaking world. Service spelled the lake's name differently for the purpose of rhyming when he wrote:

> The Northern Lights have seen queer sights,
> But the queerest they ever did see
> Was that night on the marge* of Lake Lebarge
> I cremated Sam McGee.

*shoreline

lakes during the ice ages. Among the plants that can be seen here are relatively rare species such as Baikal sedge, Yukon lupine, and blue-eyed Mary. Lodgepole pine, trembling aspens, and grey-leaved willows also manage a foothold in the sand. The wind is slowly moving the dunes and they have begun to engulf a spruce forest in one area and a playground in the town of Carcross in another.

Most of the rest of the Yukon's plateaus and valleys are covered with forests of trees such as white spruce, aspen, balsam, and pine. "Pines and pines and the shadow of pines as far as the eye can see,"[7] wrote Robert Service a century ago, describing this part of the territory. At higher elevations in the south, central, and eastern Yukon, the alpine fir grows abundantly. Willow and the shrub birch grow along the northern boundary.

All trees grow slowly in the Yukon because of the low rainfall, the short growing season, and the thin soil. For instance, it takes a coniferous tree about fifty years to reach maturity, nearly twice as long as in southern climates. Despite the challenging environment, the Yukon is nevertheless rich in forests that provide a home for the Yukon's many animal species.

Profuse Wildlife

Among the animals that inhabit the Yukon's forests and icy northern regions are three species of bears. Thousands of black bears spend their lives here, foraging for roots, tree buds, berries, and insects. Common throughout most of the Yukon, each black bear stakes out its own wandering territory of approximately 75 square miles (200 square kilometers).

Grizzly bears are also widely dispersed throughout the Yukon, but with higher concentrations in the southern areas. There are about seven thousand grizzlies in the Yukon. Polar bears number only a few hundred, and they dwell only in the most northerly regions of the Yukon.

The Yukon also provides a rich habitat for many other land-dwelling mammals. It is estimated that there are about 200,000 caribou in the territory today. Most of the herds are woodland caribou, found mainly throughout the southern half of the Yukon. Other species of mammals include the wood bison, wolves, moose, musk ox, cougar, and various species of rodents.

Approximately 214 bird species also live in the Yukon. Most of the area's breeding birds are migratory and, because of the short summers, are extremely fast at mating, laying their eggs, and raising their young. Shortly after arriving each year, these birds must quickly prepare to make the long flights

■ *The bison (left) and the moose (above) are two of the Yukon's many species of mammal.*

■ A Mammoth Find

One of the most remarkable woolly mammoth skeletons ever recovered was found near the Whitestone River in Yukon Territory's Ogilvie Mountains. This is one of the few areas in northern Canada that was not covered by the most recent ice sheet. The area was thought to provide a refuge for these huge relatives of the elephant, noted for their enormous, ten-foot-long curved tusks (often turned into jewelry by native artists) and shaggy appearance. Woolly mammoths fed on dry grasses, crunching huge daily amounts with their massive molars. Mammoth skeletons and tusks are found regularly in the riverbeds of the Klondike area. In the Siberian area of northern Russia, researchers recently recovered an almost intact specimen, frozen solid for millennia. The Whitestone River skeleton has been dated to approximately 30,000 years ago. The last of the woolly mammoths are thought to have died with the retreat of the most recent continental ice sheet circa 10,000 to 12,000 years ago.

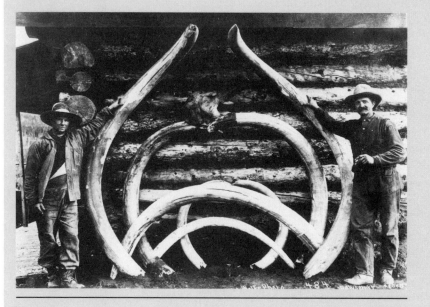

■ *Two men pose proudly with a cache of woolly mammoth tusks unearthed in the Yukon.*

back to warmer, more southerly locations. Among the migrating species are numerous waterbirds such as loons, mergansers, and arctic terns. Wetlands provide a breeding ground for up to half a million of these waterbirds each year.

A few different species of salmon also have migration routes through the Yukon waters. The many rivers and few lakes are home to about forty fish species including the arctic grayling and the northern pike.

Rivers and Lakes

The Yukon has a number of major rivers but one is a superstar among ordinary players: the Yukon River, from which the territory takes its name. The name Yukon itself comes from an Athapaskan word, Yu-kun-ah, which means "Great River." The Yukon is approximately 2,000 miles (3,200 kilometers) long, flowing from its source in British Columbia across southwestern Yukon Territory to its mouth in Alaska. It is the third-largest river in North America (after the Mississippi/Missouri and Mackenzie Rivers) and served as the main highway through the territory for native inhabitants for thousands of years. The Yukon River was the main route from Whitehorse to Dawson for the tens of thousands of gold seekers who rushed into the territory in the late 1890s. Later, with the arrival of settlers from

■ A Yukon River Disaster

In 1906, a paddle-wheeled riverboat named the *Columbian* was carrying 3 tons (2,700 kilograms) of gunpowder to the mining camps near Dawson. As it rounded a bend near Eagles Nest Bluff, a young deck boy named Phil Murray grabbed his rifle and started shooting at a flock of ducks. An older man asked for the weapon, and as the boy was handing it over, he tripped and the gun discharged right into the explosives. The entire load exploded and six crewmen were killed, including the boy. It was the worst paddle-wheel accident in Yukon's history, and Yukoners still talk about the disaster.

■ *Two paddle-wheeled boats dock along the Yukon River.*

other parts of North America, the native canoes traveling up and down the river were joined by paddleboats carrying new pioneers and supplies.

Today, most people travel by plane or they drive along the Yukon's roads and highways. "The Yukon is no longer the great artery of the north,"[8] laments Canadian author Pierre Berton. But in the summertime, locals and tourists alike still love to take a breathtaking 400-mile (650-kilometer) trip along the Yukon River. The usual route begins near Lake Laberge and ends at Dawson.

Lake Laberge is just one of southern Yukon's several lakes that were formed by the movement of glaciers pushing south during the ice ages. Yukon lakes such as Teslin, Frances, Kluane, and Tagish are narrow in shape, oriented north to south, and usually quite deep, allowing them to store significant amounts of water. Conversely, northern Yukon has fewer lakes because the permafrost limits groundwater storage.

Permafrost and Polygons

The Yukon Territory lies entirely within the northern permafrost region. Here, the upper surface of the ground, known as the active layer, thaws only in the summertime. In the southern Yukon area, the active layer can be as deep as 5 feet (1.5 meters). In the northern Yukon area, it might be only 6 to 12 inches (15 to 30 centimeters) deep. Below this active layer lies permafrost, also to varying depths. North of the Yukon's Porcupine River, the ground may be frozen more than 330 feet (100 meters) deep. The northern tip of the Yukon is also beyond the tree line, which marks the transition from forest to tundra.

When the active layer of permafrost thaws, the result is wet, marshy ground that creates a lot of water pooling. The constant freezing and thawing action causes the formation of ice-filled fissures that are outlined in ridges. These fissures form into polygons that can measure 50 to 100 feet (15 to 30 meters) across. It takes hundreds of years for these shapes to form, and they occur in large clusters. To people in airplanes, they appear to be hundreds of small lakes arranged in patterns. Tourists delight in the visual wonder of these geometric marvels.

Land of the Northern Lights

Another haunting display of nature's grandeur is the northern lights, the rippling band of colors sometimes seen in the sky of the far north. People who live in Carmacks and Faro,

and any place north of these communities, are frequently treated to this magnificent spectacle during the winter. (The night sky in the Yukon is usually too light to see the northern lights in the summer.) The scientific name for the phenomena is the aurora borealis, and the origin of this wonder is our sun. When it erupts in solar flares, charged particles project outward, and some of them penetrate the earth's upper atmosphere and are pulled to the poles. These particles react with oxygen and nitrogen to release their energy, creating the colorful lights. Atmospheric gases, weather, and other factors determine the exact colors.

People often say that photographs and films do not do justice to the phenomenon. Author Walter R. Hamilton, upon witnessing the lights, described his feelings in 1964: "dancing with quiet whispering, swooshing sounds in measured harmony, like living things, in the midst of a surrounding golden

■ *The rippled surface of the Donjek Glacier in Kluane Park. Glaciers are slow-moving sheets of ice that can dam rivers to form lakes.*

glow, seemed to spring from the very snow. . . . It seemed as if something heavenly had come down to earth in wondrous glowing light."[9]

The northern lights are just one small part of the untamed beauty of this rugged land, a land that continues to challenge inhabitants today with its rough terrain and climate. In accepting that challenge and making a life in this territory, Yukoners find an uncommon grandeur in the wilderness, and they feel a sense of belonging to such a degree that they usually refer to the rest of the world simply as "the outside." For the people of the Yukon, the territory is a special place unlike any other.

The First Nations and Fur Traders

The First Nations of the Yukon, who today still number about 20 percent of the territory's population, have long strived to live in harmony with both the land and with other peoples. Unlike in many other parts of North America, the arrival of European explorers, traders, and settlers to the Yukon did not result in violent conflict and the almost total destruction of native societies. Historians have presented a number of theories to explain why the Yukon enjoyed relative peace between natives and whites. One theory points to the especially harsh environment, which may have made it necessary for settlers to seek the help of the native peoples merely to survive. Other historians have speculated that the natives had only enough time to hunt for food before the freezing winter set in, and therefore tried to avoid conflicts as much as possible. For whatever reasons, the Yukon's First Nations developed the ability to get along with others, a respect for the land, and a belief in self-determinism that remain alive today.

Out of Asia

One reason that the Yukon's native peoples considered harmony with the land so important is that they believed they were a part of the land's creation, and that their ancestors had lived there since that creation. Their myths and legends, passed on orally from generation to generation, described

■ *The Friendship totem pole of the Yukon city of Whitehorse. Native peoples of the region use totem poles to represent family lineages and mythical incidents.*

how a raven transformed a world of water into land they could inhabit.

Some modern archaeologists believe that there is a germ of truth in these old stories. Some ten thousand to twelve thousand years ago, upon the retreat of the last great ice sheet that covered much of Canada, the land bridge that once connected Alaska and Asia was flooded by rising waters in the Pacific Ocean and the Bering Sea, breaking the solid link between the two continents. But for thousands of years before that, the earliest inhabitants of North America had been crossing that land bridge, migrating from Asia into present-day Alaska, the Yukon, and points south and east, eventually reaching all the way down into South America.

Over the span of hundreds of generations, distinct native groups formed among the peoples who inhabited the Yukon. A number of these tribes, including the Tutchone, Kaska, and Tagish, shared a language as well as cultural traits now identified as Athapaskan. In the far northern reaches of the territory, the Inuit (Eskimo) developed a distinct First Nations society based on hunting seals, walrus, and caribou.

A final First Nations people, the Tlingit, did not arrive until relatively recently, drawn by their interactions with the earliest fur traders. The Tlingit filtered into southern Yukon Territory from the coastal areas of present-day Alaska and British Columbia, where the headwaters of the Yukon River are surrounded by forests and lakes. This coastal location proved ideal for the Tlingit, for they enjoyed an abundance of natural resources and established themselves in permanent villages. The Tlingit fished for salmon and hunted small game as well as moose and caribou. They also developed a strong trade, offering coveted items such as shells, dried foods, wooden boxes, and candlefish oil.

Early Athapaskan Societies

While archaeologists are still researching Tlingit life prior to the arrival of Europeans, more is known about the Athapaskan groups that lived in the inland regions of the Yukon. In this subarctic landscape, ancient campsites and Athapaskan

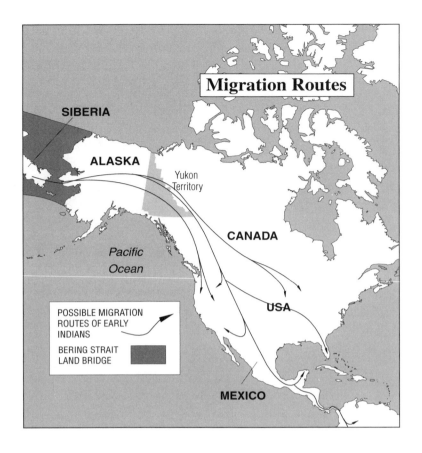

artifacts have been uncovered that provide clues about natives' early history and lifestyle. The evidence indicates that after settling in an area, a group of Athapaskan would claim the territory as their own. Thus, for example, the Tagish were concentrated around lakes and rivers in the southeast section of the Yukon, and the Tutchone in the west, from the area of today's Kluane National Park north to Dawson.

Athapaskan tribes mostly following a seminomadic way of life best described as "restricted wandering." They would set up temporary camps to seek food and other needed supplies. But as the food never lasted long in one place, they soon had to move on for their continued survival. As different specialized handiwork skills developed within one Athapaskan group or another, they often traded skills. As such, a sort of cultural diversity often evolved, with different groups taking on unique characteristics.

In general, Athapaskan lifestyle called for familiarity with the land and careful attention to the changing seasons. In the summer, some bands would gather at large fish camps. The

■ *Tlingit societies shared hunting and fishing techniques with their northern neighbor the Inuit (pictured).*

■ Living Off the Land

Living in so northern a territory, with little land suitable for farming and such a short growing season, the tribes native to the Yukon had to develop superior skills in hunting and seasonal foraging. When fall came, the large bands split into smaller groups, usually based on the extended family. This allowed them to go their separate ways to hunt and find enough food to support the smaller group. What each small family group hunted largely depended upon the location and its wildlife. Differing resources led to varied strategies for hunting and fishing from one group to another. Some of the more common animals they hunted, however, were beavers, caribou, bears, Dall sheep, mountain goats, moose, ducks, and geese. Many groups would also trap small animals like hares and rabbits.

In summer, the women would collect wild berries such as mossberries, cranberries, raspberries, stoneberries, and blueberries, all of which they dried for winter storage. Sometimes berry-picking women had to compete with bears for the same food. In order to keep the bears away, the women would stay in groups, talking very loudly and singing. The women also foraged for mushrooms and wild onions.

■ *Raspberries are one of the seasonal foods for which women of the Yukon tribes foraged.*

men fished with nets and willow traps, or they would simply spear the fish. Meanwhile, the women cleaned and dried the fish for winter. Often in summer, bands also traveled down the rivers in canoes made from sewn birch bark, cedar bark, or moose hide. On these journeys, they searched for edible berries as well as medicinal leaves and roots. Sometimes one or two family groups would join together to travel to where the caribou lived. When the people arrived, they would build a pole house covered with moss and soil.

Summer was the one season of plenty for the Athapaskan. During the summer months, they lived in lean-to shelters made from animal skins. Such shelters were portable and allowed them to travel easily, so they could also visit other villages to trade in mountain goat hair, raw copper, and hides. But Yukon summers do not last long, and when colder weather arrived, food would become scarce. There would not be enough to go around for a large group all situated in one place.

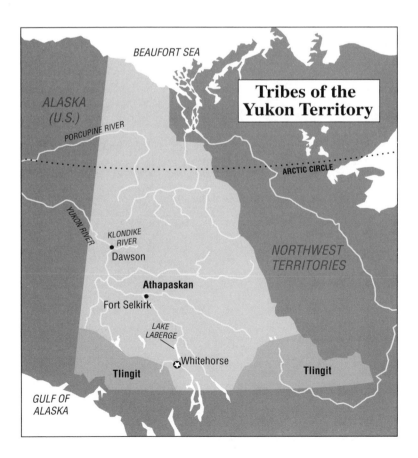

■ *A caribou cow an-
nounces her presence.*

Hunting Caribou

Caribou usually proved to be an excellent source of food during cold weather. In part this was because a number of Athapaskan groups developed an efficient method of trapping a large number of caribou at one time using specially constructed fences. These fences consisted of posts made from tree branches, which were planted in the ground forming a long—up to 2 miles (3 kilometers)—funnel-shaped V. A caribou herd would enter the trap at the wide end. Stampeded by shouts from the Athapaskan, the animals would find themselves packed closer and closer, unable to turn around or get out because of the charging animals behind them. At the point of the V, a corral was erected where the hunters would snare the trapped animals using large nooses made of animal hide. They would then kill the caribou with spears or with bows and arrows.

The Athapaskan had a deep respect for the caribou. It was unthinkable to the Athapaskan that any part of the animal would be wasted after it was killed. Any meat that was not immediately eaten would be dried or smoked to preserve it for future use. The hides were used to make warm clothing and shelter. Caribou skin lacings made snowshoes that allowed travel in the deep snow of winter. And the horns, bones, hooves, and intestines were used to make items such as weapons, scrapers, needles, and various tools.

Season by Season

Despite native societies' hunting skills and ingenuity, however, as winter progressed, their food stores would eventually start to deplete. The animals became scarcer, and the ones natives did manage to kill were thinner with less meat on them. This would mean that it was time to move on and adopt different survival tactics. The men in the small groups would then set out on their own in search of rabbits, moose, or wintering birds. During this time, they traveled lightly, with just their weapons and a small shelter. This allowed them to search for food over greater distances.

Meanwhile, the women had the job of packing up all the group's belongings and carrying everything to the next camp, where the men would ultimately meet up with them. If luck was with the family group, the survival skills passed down from generation to generation allowed everyone to make it through the harsh winter.

But the end of winter hardly meant that natives' difficulties were over. The short spring in the Yukon was generally the hardest time for the Athapaskan because by then, the remaining stores of food had usually run out. Although migrating waterfowl were already beginning to return to the region, the melting ice on the rivers made travel extremely arduous and even dangerous, hindering spring hunting. So those last days before the summer months—the months when there would again be an abundance of food and when the people could once again come together as a large social group at one of the fishing camps—usually proved the most trying of all.

■ *A Canadian Indian poses for a portrait.*

Individuals Make the Group

The social lifestyles in First Nations villages closely echoed those of family life. There was no set political system and no formal methods for enforcing laws. Survival of the group, as well as the family, depended on the commitment and contribution of each individual, which encouraged self-initiative. Strong individuals made for a strong group. Leadership was bestowed on individuals according to their skills for the job at hand. One man could be a trading leader, another a hunting leader, and yet another might be a spiritual leader, or a shaman.

The women also had different roles. Some were, for instance, the teachers and storytellers. Storytelling was an important part of the social culture because the stories were rich with wisdom. Many tales taught lessons about survival skills, social customs, or the ability to adapt to the environment that needed to be passed down through the generations.

A World Populated by Spirits

The Athapaskan ideal of independence and self-reliance carried over into their religious principles as well. For them, spirituality was as much a part of survival as were the other individual skills they developed. This meant that each person was encouraged to develop his or her own ideas and rituals relating to the supernatural. Some people believed that spirits

■ *A Tlingit rattle with raven, shaman, frog, and totemic wolf face.*

lived in another world, and only sometimes visited the human world. Others believed that spirits lived in the everyday world, but lurked in hidden areas. In either case, if a person wanted to have an easy life, it was important to behave well. Otherwise, the spirits might intervene and cause difficulties. Good behavior often translated to a life of moderation. If one were to overeat, for example, it was thought that he or she would surely starve in the future. If a person were vain, this would bring on an injury that would make that person ugly.

Such beliefs were reinforced by the shamans, who were recognized as having especially close relationships with the spirit world. Through dreams, songs, dances, and potions, they provided the people with guidance and medical services. Some tribes believed that shamans' powers extended to changing the weather and predicting the movements of game.

Spiritual beliefs were engrained in everyday life. For example, it was generally believed that an animal's spirit could either help a hunter or could prevent the animal's death. In other words, it was not possible to kill an animal that had decided not to die. A hunter must therefore show proper respect to the animal even after he killed it.

■ A Rite of Passage

Young Athapaskan men were sometimes sent out into the wilderness to find their spirit helpers. The young men were expected to fast and show courage. Through dreams, they would bond with their animal spirit helpers. The young men were often given the gift of a song or a special chant that would later work as a charm against any potential trouble. Sometimes, a man would have more than one spirit helper. In fact, the more spirit helpers a man could acquire, the more influential he became within his clan. Women sometimes found their spirit helpers when they reached childbearing years. Most often, though, women did not depend on spirit helpers and learned to survive by their wits.

Spiritual views of animals even in-
fluenced First Nations marriage rituals.
Athapaskan groups divided their people
into two clans, Wolf and Crow. Babies
were born into one or the other, depending upon the clan of the mother. This
meant that the animal spirit was handed
down from mother to children. Then,
according to tradition, Crow women
must marry Wolf men, and Wolf women
must marry Crow men. This clan identity remained strong even as European
culture began to expand into the area of
the Yukon.

Contact with Europeans

Long before most of the First Nations
people in the present-day Yukon ever saw
Europeans, the natives felt settlers' reach
in the New World. By the late 1700s,
trade networks had already been established between European and native
groups in other parts of North America.

■ *Animal pelts and other goods on display at a Yukon trading post.*

Besides bringing goods to trade, the Europeans also brought
diseases like smallpox. Because the Europeans had been exposed to these diseases for centuries, they had developed
some measure of immunity. Native groups, however, had no
immunity and diseases such as smallpox often wiped out entire tribes. Sickness spread between trading natives and
quickly reached as far as the Yukon even before white men appeared in the area. The number of deaths in the nineteenth
century among the Yukon's Athapaskan and Tlingit due to
European diseases is not known. Even when tribes survived, it
was often the elders who succumbed. The death of elders
could be an overwhelming loss to a society that relied on its
oral traditions. The native people often blamed the scourge
on angry spirits or the shamans.

The first direct contact between Europeans and Yukon Indians probably occurred in the first decades of the nineteenth
century when Tlingit groups began trading with Russians.
The Russians had set up posts on the coastal islands of present-
day Alaska to take advantage of what seemed to be an almost
inexhaustible supply of animal pelts. Sea otters in particular
were highly valued for their warm fur. Russian and other European traders had discovered, as they explored the frontier

regions of North America, that natives could often be persuaded to exchange an entire winter's catch of furs for European goods, such as metal pots, beads, blankets, alcohol, and guns. Such manufactured goods eventually made their way to Athapaskan groups who traded with the Tlingit.

The First Europeans Arrive

Russian claims to a large but vaguely defined part of northwestern North America angered the British, who considered the Yukon theirs. The Hudson's Bay Company had been established in 1670 when the king of England, Charles II, gave a group of British noblemen a charter granting them a complete monopoly on the fur trade—as well as governing power—in a large part of North America around the Hudson Bay. Later, in 1821, when the Hudson's Bay Company merged with its rival, the North West Company, that fur-trading monopoly was extended to almost all the lands the British controlled, including the huge area drained by the Yukon River. At this time the Hudson's Bay Company appointed the Scotsman George Simpson as governor of its vast Northern Department, which included the area of the Yukon.

In the early 1820s the Hudson's Bay Company had not yet established an outpost in the Yukon, nor even begun to trade there. Simpson nevertheless demanded that the Russians cease their fur trade. To prevent an escalating conflict, a treaty was drawn up between the Russians and British in 1825. The Russians mainly wanted to be able to trade along the coastal areas of present-day British Columbia and Alaska for sea otter, and the British wanted a monopoly on furs in the Yukon interior for the Hudson's Bay Company. So the treaty gave each what they wanted most.

The first European to set foot in the present-day Yukon Territory was probably a member of an expedition led by the ill-fated British explorer John Franklin. A party under his command explored the route up the Mackenzie River from Great Slave Lake in present-day Northwest Territories from 1825 to 1827. At the Mackenzie's mouth in the Beaufort Sea of the Arctic Ocean, Franklin's group explored west along the shoreline of what later became Yukon Territory and Alaska. Franklin was to die some twenty years later, along with 128 of his men, when ships he was commanding in a search for the Northwest Passage became stuck in Arctic ice. (The Northwest Passage was a sea route across the top of Canada, from the Atlantic to the Pacific, long sought by European powers as a shortcut to Asia.)

■ *Yukon natives pose in front of Fort Selkirk, an important Hudson's Bay Company trading post.*

Fur Trade from the East and South

Still, by the 1830s European fur traders had yet to explore the mountainous areas north of present-day British Columbia. The Hudson's Bay Company had, however, recognized the importance of the Mackenzie River as a fur-trading route. In 1839 a party of explorers led by Hudson's Bay Company officer John Bell journeyed south from the point where the Peel River empties into the Mackenzie, in present-day Northwest Territories. Bell and his men went down the Peel and then the Snake River, in present-day Yukon Territory. He reported back that the area was rich in animals and fish, leading the company in 1840 to establish a fort on the lower Peel.

In the south, the Athapaskan were receiving Russian manufactured goods from the Tlingit in exchange for their furs, and they wanted more. So they sent Athapaskan representatives to the distant Peel River Trading Post (today's Fort McPherson in the Northwest Territories) to urge the Hudson's Bay Company to come to the area of the Yukon River to trade directly with them. This sounded like a good idea to the Hudson's Bay Company, which was constantly extending its trading operations in search of higher profits.

In 1847, the geologist and explorer Alexander Murray led a party to the junction of the Yukon and Porcupine Rivers, where they built Fort Youcon for the Hudson's Bay Company. Although this was in present-day Alaska, and presumably outside the jurisdiction of the company, it was so far from the nearest Russian post in Nulato (700 miles, or 1,100 kilometers, downriver) that the Russians simply ignored the fort.

In 1848, Robert Campbell of the Hudson's Bay Company arrived at the junction of the Pelly and Yukon Rivers and set up a fur-trading post called Fort Selkirk. This was a long-awaited occasion for the Athapaskan, but the Tlingit resented this intrusion on the trading monopoly that they had established with the interior natives. In 1852, the Tlingit attacked the post and took all the goods, although they left the white traders unharmed. This was enough for the Hudson's Bay Company to decide to abandon Fort Selkirk. Later, the Athapaskan burned it down in order to get the iron fittings from the wood and use them for tools.

Natives Become Trade Partners

The Hudson's Bay Company then concentrated on the trade downriver at Fort Youcon. Trading with the Athapaskan, however, proved to be an ongoing challenge for the company men, who were not used to natives dictating trading terms and even using trickery to get what they wanted. The Athapaskans' most desired trading goods were guns to make hunting easier and beads to decorate their clothing. Upon learning of this, the company insisted that these items could be traded only for white fox and marten, which were the most valuable pelts. Native groups then refused any trade at all unless all of their pelts were accepted in exchange for the goods. They would even travel the great distance to the Alaska coast and trade with the Russians just to spite the Hudson's Bay Company. Using tactics like these, the First Nations retained control of the fur trade.

Fort Youcon was remote, far from the Hudson's Bay Company's Montreal-area headquarters over a long and difficult supply route. In addition to being vulnerable and weak, the fort was operating illegally in Russian territory. The Athapaskan took full advantage of this. On one occasion, they told the men at Fort Youcon that the Russians had armed a boat with a cannon and were planning to sail up the Yukon River to drive the British out of Alaska. The Hudson's Bay Company eventually discovered this was completely untrue, but the threat did result in extracting better trading terms from the company for a while.

This uneasy give-and-take between the Athapaskan and the Hudson's Bay Company lasted for decades. Each needed and learned from the other. Despite the ups and downs of their business dealings, the traders and the natives did share much in common, including the tough challenge of simply staying alive in a harsh land.

The fur traders recognized that the native culture had already mastered survival skills, and many Europeans embraced a great deal of the native lifestyle. As was true for the natives, much of the traders' time and effort was devoted to hunting moose, bear, and caribou for meat, and to drying and storing this meat for winter. Traders also chopped and stacked large amounts of firewood in preparation for cold weather, when temperatures would drop as low as −50°F (−45°C). Salmon had to be caught and dried or bought from the natives who fished in the summer. Often traders would even marry native women. Likewise, the Athapaskan acquired bits of European culture and learned to use various manufactured goods.

Decline of the Fur Trade

It is not surprising that both the British and Athapaskan came to depend on each other to make the Yukon fur trade work— a trade that was never all that profitable for the Hudson's Bay Company. The problem was that the furs had to be transported a considerable distance east, along rivers and even overland, before they could be loaded on large ships bound for Britain and elsewhere. So to make any profit at all, the company needed the natives' cooperation.

Despite the constant threats by the Athapaskan to trade with the Russians, the Athapaskan wanted and preferred the higher-quality British trade goods. So most of the time, business between the Athapaskan and the company men at Fort Youcon continued as a yearly routine. By the 1860s, political developments were curtailing the Hudson's Bay Company fur trade. In 1867, Russia sold Alaska, including Fort Youcon (now Fort Yukon), to the United States. And in 1869, the new Dominion of Canada purchased the Hudson's Bay Company's North American land holdings.

When the Hudson's Bay Company finally abandoned its posts, most natives easily returned to their traditional lifestyles. Unlike the natives in other parts of Canada, they had not become full-time hunters for the company, and for the most part they had not moved into camps near trading posts. The introduction of items such as guns, flour, cloth, and metal pots and pans had slightly altered their ways. More changes, however, were on the horizon.

■ *A canoe of European voyagers manned by Indians. The canoe brought Europeans to the more remote areas of the Yukon.*

Mining for Souls and Gold

During the latter half of the nineteenth century, the Yukon remained a mostly unexplored and unsettled land. In the 1870s, two new groups of Europeans began to trickle into the area from northern British Columbia, which had become a province of the new country of Canada in 1871. One group was Christian missionaries. The Roman Catholic Church and the Anglican Church of England were competing with each other at the time to convert as many New World natives as possible. This rivalry caused an obsessive drive to convince the native peoples in the Yukon that only by converting to the Christian faith could their souls be saved.

Both the Catholics and Anglicans tried to impose their beliefs on the natives and convince them to abandon their own spiritual practices, which were based on a harmonious balance with nature. The missionaries also set up and ran the first native schools in the area of the Yukon. The purpose of the schools, they said, was to rid the natives of their "unwholesomeness" and to replace it with "the blessings of civilization."[10] The native children learned reading, writing, and basic math, but the schools also turned them away from their families and traditions. This ultimately proved to be a tragedy, as Minister of the Interior Frank Oliver noted in 1908: "To teach an Indian child that his parents are degraded beyond measure and that whatever they did or thought was wrong could only result in the child becoming . . . admittedly and unquestionably very much less desirable a member of society than their parents, who never saw the schools."[11]

The missionaries' influence was persistent but it was the other group of newcomers in the late nineteenth century—prospectors in search of gold—that was to have the greatest impact on the future of the area.

Gold Brings Territorial Status

Τhe promise of handsome profits—and eventually even fortunes—had originally brought Europeans and other white people to the rugged Yukon region, first as a trickle and then as a raging flood. From the mid-1700s to the beginning of the 1900s, the Yukon was viewed by whites as a wild land to be plundered of its valuable natural resources. As the fur trade was declining, another of the Yukon's natural resources was rapidly becoming the central preoccupation of most white people in the region. That natural resource was gold.

Rumors of Gold

Stories about gold in the tributaries of the Yukon River had been circulating among fur traders since the 1860s. Major gold rushes had occurred in California after a strike in 1848 and in British Columbia after a strike in 1858. Savvy fur traders and prospectors thought the Yukon might be next, but the area remained remote and mostly still unexplored. Fur traders in particular were not eager to publicize rumors of gold, since they feared that if news got out, it might disrupt the fur trade. Leroy Napoleon McQuesten, a farm boy from New England who worked for the Hudson's Bay Company for a time, wrote of one story he heard that indicated that the Hudson's Bay men knew about gold, but were trying to keep quiet about it:

■ *A team of gold miners poses at the entrance to a mining shaft.*

One of the officers [of the Hudson's Bay Company] that came up on the steamer washed out a jar of dirt near Fort Yukon and he had about a teaspoonful of something yellow in the pan and the officer threw it away remarking that it would not do to let the men see it as they would all leave the steamer. . . . By the way the officer acted trying to hide it from the other men he supposed it must be gold.[12]

Rumors of gold did continue to circulate nevertheless and began to draw a few prospectors from the coast. In the summer of 1881, four men—Arthur Harper, a man known only as Bates, and two natives—hiked over the highlands north of the coastal mountains into the region of Alaska's Tanana River to prospect. As they crossed one small river, the swift current swept Bates off his feet and he nearly drowned. While he dried his clothes, Harper collected a sample of sand.

Bates stored this sample along with others the group had taken, and later when he left the Yukon and returned to San Francisco, he had the sample analyzed. It was rich in gold—the equivalent of $20,000 worth per ton of sand, a huge fortune in those days. He told Harper of their find, but when Harper returned to the Tanana River region, he could no longer find the spot where he had collected the gold-rich sample.

A Strike in the Klondike

More than a decade later, during the summer of 1896, prospector Robert Henderson of Nova Scotia scooped up a pan of gravel and sand from the bed of a remote creek not far from the junction of the Yukon and Klondike Rivers. He grew excited when he found precious flakes of gold and dubbed the stream Gold Bottom Creek. "This prospector was an important but unlucky character in the story of the Klondike Gold Rush," wrote author Michael Cooper. He notes that after the

---

■ The Sourdoughs

During the Klondike days, many goods were in short supply. One of the most difficult items to find was baker's yeast, a necessary ingredient for the baking of good quality breads and pastries. The gold miners, who so often had to make do with what they had, created a type of bread that was made without baker's yeast. They called it sourdough. Flour and water, along with rice water and a pinch of sugar, were put in a pail and hung over a stove or fire where it would be kept warm for hours. The presence of naturally occurring wild yeasts caused fermentation and made the bread rise a little. In the late 1800s, the Klondikers also began calling themselves Sourdoughs. The term referred to someone who had become wise in the ways of Yukon life. The famous Yukon writer Robert Service helped immortalize the term by naming his first collection of poems *Songs of a Sourdough*. Some Yukon old-timers still refer to themselves as Sourdoughs.

■ *California and Yukon gold miners developed a unique type of sourdough bread.*

Prospectors pan for gold in a creek near the Klondike River.

find, "Henderson dug feverishly for several weeks. He unearthed over $750 worth of gold flakes and nuggets. This was more money than most people in those days earned in a year."[13]

Henderson mentioned his success to another prospector, George Carmack, the son of a veteran of the California gold rush. Carmack and a pair of Tagish, Skookum Jim Mason and Tagish Charlie, had been fishing, trading furs, and prospecting with meager results for the previous three years. When the trio learned of Henderson's find, they explored a Klondike tributary called Rabbit Creek that they thought especially promising. Sure enough, on August 17, 1896, they found small nuggets and flakes of gold just waiting to be plucked from the cold water. Carmack, Skookum Jim, and Charlie quickly registered their claim along the renamed Bonanza Creek. News spread rapidly to the nearby town of Fortymile, which emptied almost overnight as townsfolk rushed to stake their own claims. Other prospectors quickly filed claims along nearby Eldorado Creek, which eventually proved to be an even richer source of gold. Unfortunately for Henderson, the stream he had staked out never yielded much more gold.

The Klondike discovery set off the last great gold rush of North America. The town of Dawson City, which was named after George Dawson of the Geological Survey of Canada, sprouted up near the junction of the Yukon and Klondike Rivers. Within two years it would hold a staggering thirty thousand people. The great Klondike gold rush had begun.

The News Spreads

Overnight, the discovery of gold changed the Yukon. Word sifted south even as men scrambled north. As Canadian author Pierre Berton colorfully described the process:

> Up and down the Yukon Valley the news spread like a great stage-whisper. It moved as swiftly as the breeze in the birches, and more mysteriously. Men squatting by nameless creeks heard the tale, dropped their pans, and headed for the Klondike. Men seated by dying campfires heard it and started up in the night, shrugging off sleep to make tracks for the new strike. Men poling up the Yukon towards the mountains or drifting down the Yukon towards the wilderness heard it and did an abrupt about-face in the direction of the salmon stream whose name no one could pronounce properly. Some did not hear the news at all, but, drifting past the Klondike's mouth, saw the boats and the tents and the gesticulating figures, felt the hair rise on their napes, and then, still uncomprehending, still unbelieving, joined the clamoring throng pushing up through the weeds and the muck of Rabbit Creek.[14]

It took some time, however, for the news to reach California and points east, mostly because of how isolated the Yukon was from the rest of the world. In early 1897, word about the gold rush had not yet leaked out beyond the Yukon and Alaska. By then, most of the good claims had already been staked. It was not until eleven months after the Rabbit Creek strike that the outside world first learned of the new golden opportunities awaiting in the Yukon. After the spring thaw in 1897, about eighty of the newly wealthy prospectors headed back to the Alaska coast to return to civilization. These men each carried with them a fortune in gold, from $25,000 to $500,000 worth of gold stuffed in anything they could lay their hands on—suitcases, boxes, old cans, jam jars, medicine bottles, and sacks made from caribou hides.

The lucky prospectors boarded two coastal steamers, the *Excelsior* bound for San Francisco and the *Portland* headed to Seattle. When these boats reached their destinations in mid-July 1897, a media frenzy ensued. Newspapers from around the world rushed to cover this story of fabulous riches waiting to be found in the Yukon.

The Rush North

Gold fever swept across North America. The mineral madness was in many ways even more intense than earlier gold rushes, perhaps because much of the world's economy was suffering from a severe depression at the time. Many men and women

■ *Armed with a shotgun, a Yukon gold prospector poses with his pack mule and dog.*

were having trouble earning enough to simply feed themselves. And here were true tales of men who had become wealthy overnight.

Thousands immediately tried to book passage on any boat headed to the Yukon. Across North America, people from all walks of life quit their jobs, abandoned their families or dragged them along, and started a mad race for the Klondike to get rich. In Canada, many of these people headed to Edmonton or Vancouver as stepping-stones to the Yukon. The populations of both of these towns doubled during the rush.

The long and difficult journey from Edmonton, which went north mostly by river almost to the Beaufort Sea and then turned west to go overland across mountains, came to be known as the Klondike Trail. Gold seekers often took months to negotiate it. An estimated 1,600 prospectors set off down the Klondike Trail but fewer than half actually made it all the way to the Yukon. Most turned back or stayed in Alberta or British Columbia, though thirty-five died along the route. Horses were even unluckier—of the thousands that set off along the Klondike Trail, not a single one apparently made it to Dawson City.

The much more popular route was by sea and then overland. An estimated 100,000 people set sail for the Yukon gold fields from 1897 until the rush ended seven years later. By August 1897, steamships from Victoria, Seattle, and San Francisco arrived almost every day at Skagway, the Alaska boomtown that served as the trailhead for the main routes into the Yukon.

Inland from Skagway

Skagway, tucked into the panhandle about 100 miles (160 kilometers) north of Juneau, is where the "Inside Passage" ends. This is the sheltered sea route that winds among the is-

lands of the British Columbia and Alaska coasts all the way from Vancouver Island. In the 1890s, two main trails took off from Skagway and passed through the thin strip of British Columbia before entering the Yukon. These were both tough trails, however, as they had to cover the rugged terrain of the Coast Mountains, which harbors some of the highest peaks in North America. Even after making it to Bennett, British Columbia, some 50 miles (80 kilometers) as the crow flies from Skagway, gold seekers still faced the long, 500-mile (800-kilometer) trip down the Yukon River. Many a ramshackle raft was built to float down the Yukon, past Whitehorse and on to Dawson and the Klondike gold fields. Rapids near Whitehorse and elsewhere claimed dozens of these crafts and more than a few lives.

The Chilkoot Trail from Skagway to Bennett was especially tough because it was too steep for horses and wagons. Thus, most miners had to carry their supplies on their backs. The Northwest Mounted Police, a federal police force Canada organized in 1873, was enlisted to help enforce a government rule requiring prospectors to pack a year's worth of supplies, which in total weighed almost a ton. The Mounties thus established a checkpoint on the Chilkoot. Prospectors could carry only about sixty pounds at a time, so many made repeated trips over the Chilkoot, lugging everything from socks and blankets to food and utensils. Others gave up without ever reaching the Yukon.

■ *A team of gold prospectors leaves Juneau, Alaska, headed for the Yukon.*

■ Mounties Keep the Peace

In spite of the huge numbers of people who streamed into the Yukon, the Klondike was the most peaceful gold rush in North American history. To a large extent, this was due to the excellent work of the Northwest Mounted Police, who allowed none of the gun-slinging violence that had been common in the California gold rush of the early 1850s. The Mounties helped to make sure that the claims the prospectors staked were properly marked, filed, and recorded, greatly reducing the potential for violent feuds. As a result, most of the prospectors, a majority of whom were American, came to respect Canadian law and abide by it.

Dawson, for instance, was a remarkably tame town due to the two hundred Northwest Mounted Police garrisoned there to maintain strict law and order. No one in Dawson was permitted to carry a revolver without a license, and few were given licenses. As a result, there were only two murders and a few cases of brawling in 1898. In *Klondike Fever*, Michael Cooper quotes police inspector Samuel Steele as saying, "Acts of indecency are severely punished and it can be safely said that any man, woman, or child may walk at any time of the night to any portion of this large camp with perfect safety from insult." In all of the Yukon that year, the Mounties recorded only 137 deaths, most from disease, especially typhoid fever.

■ *Two officers of the Northwest Mounted Police ride across a meadow.*

The White Pass trail, which also ran from Skagway to Bennett, more or less paralleled the Chilkoot a little to the south. It followed a canyon route that was not as steep as the Chilkoot and horses could make their way along it. But it was longer, and muddier in wet weather, when it would become congested and nearly impassable. The deep mud made it a horror for horses and mules, especially along a section that became known as Dead Horse Gulch. Author Jack London, who traveled the White Pass in the fall of 1897, described the tragic fate of these poor pack animals:

> The horses died like mosquitoes in the first frost and from Skagway to Bennett they rotted in heaps. They died at the rocks, they were poisoned at the summit, and they starved at the lakes; they fell off the trail, what there was of it, and they went through it; in the river they drowned under their loads or were smashed to pieces against the boulders; they snapped their legs in the crevices and broke their backs falling backwards with their packs; in the sloughs they sank from fright or smothered in the slime; and they were disemboweled in the bogs where the corduroy logs turned end up in the mud; men shot them, worked them to death and when they were gone, went back to the beach and bought more.[15]

Despite the difficulties, through the winter of 1897–1898, people poured into Dawson and set out into the Yukon wilds, often terribly ill equipped and unprepared for the harsh environment, determined to find their share of the gold.

Getting the Gold

Looking for gold was simple, but it was also hard work. Prospectors would take a quantity of gravel in a pie-shaped pan about two feet in diameter, fill it half full of water, and swirl the mixture around while holding the pan angled slightly downward. The gravel would spill out of the pan in small quantities. But because gold is heavier than gravel, it remained in the pan while the lighter matter was washed out. If prospectors found small flakes of gold in the gravel that eventually remained in the pan, they would stake a claim and then dig down farther in the earth to try and find richer deposits of gold. This was where the hard work began because of conditions in the Yukon.

The Klondike River region is only about 150 miles (240 kilometers) south of the Arctic Circle. Because the cold climate causes the ground to remain permanently frozen slightly below the surface, even in midsummer, prospectors first had to thaw the ground to dig for gold. They did this by chopping down trees and building big fires. The process often had to be repeated a number of times to dig more deeply. If a gold vein was found, the prospectors would then dig horizontally, thawing the earth as they went.

All this was generally done in the winter, and the gravel was piled on the surface to wait for spring, when warm weather would completely thaw it and there were quantities of water available. The gravel was then run through a sluice box—a wooden trough roughly 6 feet (2 meters) long. Small strips of wood called "riffles" were placed across the bottom of the sluice box. As water washed the gravel down the length of the box, the gold fell to the bottom, where it was caught by the riffles. At intervals, the water was stopped and the gold was scraped off the upper edge of the riffles.

The Boom Goes Bust

In all, it is estimated that of the 100,000 people who set out for the Klondike, only about 40,000 actually managed to make it there. The rest ran out of money or the resolve to

■ *A prospector carries a load of gravel to his partner, who is panning for gold.*

carry on, became ill from the hard journey along the overland trails, or died along the way. They did not know that most of the profitable claims had already been staked by the Yukoners who had arrived there first. Thus, even among those who made it, perhaps as few as 4,000 actually found any gold with a few hundred of these lucky enough to parlay their findings into long-term wealth. Among these was George Carmack,

who moved back to the United States and was wealthy enough to leave an estate to his wife when he died in 1922. Skookum Jim and Tagish Charlie also lived lavishly for a number of years on their prospecting finds.

The U.S. mints in Seattle and San Francisco received $10 million worth of Yukon gold nuggets and dust in 1898, $16 million in 1899, and $22 million in 1900. After that, deposits fell. By 1904 the rush was over—what gold was left could be extracted from the earth only with the use of powerful machines, such as dredges. Many of the latecomers who came from outside the region ultimately returned south, no richer for their efforts.

The Yukon fur traders' early fears that a gold rush would have a negative effect upon the fur industry turned out to be legitimate. Many trappers abandoned the search for furs when gold promised much easier and quicker riches. The slowdown in the Yukon's fur trading industry was bad news for natives. After the 1890s, trading posts were often established or relocated to serve the needs of miners rather than to trade with Yukon's First Nations. The Athapaskan, who had come to depend on these posts, then had to travel longer distances to trade their furs. Many natives became what authors Ken S. Coates and William R. Morrison described as "powerless outsiders in

■ *A prospector separates gold from gravel by means of a sluice box as his partner brings bucketfuls more of the rock.*

■ *Klondike-area children pose with their dog by a street sign as a gold rush town is being erected around them.*

the economic life of their own country."[16] Of course, not all the natives did poorly during the gold rush. Although most did not actually prospect for and find gold themselves, many profited from the gold rush by selling meat and fish to the miners.

The Yukon Becomes a Territory

Gold mining remained a major industry in the region for the next half century, but it was taken over by big mining companies. By 1900 engineers had blasted through the mountains along the White Pass Trail to construct a narrow-gauge railway from Skagway to Whitehorse. The new White Pass and Yukon Railway allowed the mining companies to bring in gold dredges—large machines that allowed a few men to do what it took hundreds to do previously. The dredges could move tons of gravel in a single day. This changed not just the nature of gold mining in the region, but ultimately the governance of the region.

■ Codes of Conduct in the Wild

The Klondike gold miners came from all over North America and in some cases from Europe and even Asia. As an instant community of strangers searching for gold in the wilderness, the prospectors needed to develop their own rules and regulations to feel safe. Far from Mountie-controlled Dawson, they could not depend upon police to protect their lives and shelters. What consequently emerged were unwritten codes to live by. For instance, it was taken for granted that food and shelter would be given to any visiting stranger who asked for it. Petty theft and even selfish behavior were frowned upon and considered to be a threat to the whole community.

In order to enforce their codes of conduct, miners often met in informal councils to make decisions on all legal and social matters. Anyone with a grievance could call for a meeting that would be attended by everyone living in the area. The miners aired criminal accusations, quarrels, and disputes about mining boundaries. The accused were often judged not just on their past actions, but also on what they might be likely to do in the future. The final verdict was decided by majority vote. If the vote went against the accused, he or she often would be banished from the community. These frontier examples of town meetings were surprisingly democratic, often granting women and natives who were present an equal right to participate and vote.

As the big companies took over the mining, political changes followed. It was as a direct result of the Klondike gold rush that the Yukon, which had been made a district of the Northwest Territories in 1895, became a separate territory of the Dominion of Canada on July 13, 1898. This placed the area, where Americans had come to outnumber Canadians, firmly under the control of the Northwest Mounted Police and the federal government. Canadian officials in Ottawa appointed a commissioner and a six-member legislative council to govern the territory. The Canadian government was so keen on establishing federal authority over the area that the legislative council's early meetings were closed to the public.

In particular, the authorities were determined that Dawson City would not become a Wild West town like Skagway, as this might undermine Canadian sovereignty. Police reinforcements were rushed into the Klondike as the numbers of prospectors increased. Before gold had been discovered, the area had only about 20 police officers. This number was increased to 196, and eventually to 300, with an additional 200 soldiers from the Canadian army also stationed there from 1898 to 1900. The police worked hard to assert their authority and to maintain law and order—the main reason the town of Dawson, which eventually reached a population of forty thousand, remained so free of crime.

The tradition of competitive cooperation and of helping and respecting one's fellows, which began with the fur trade, continued on, reinforced both by the government and its policing policies.

Building a Modern Territory

M ore so than any other event in the history of the Yukon, the Klondike gold rush forever transformed the region. In the wake of a huge influx of nonnatives, the region experienced an accelerated introduction to urbanization, modern technology, environmental damage, and a number of the other trappings of the twentieth century. Before the Yukon could enjoy the fruits of modernization, however, it experienced a period of extended stagnation, a "gold rush hangover," that began during the first decade of the nineteenth century. As the Klondike gold rush wound down, the majority of European settlers began to leave the Yukon almost as eagerly as they had come. With their departure, much of the government and the social structure, and even some of the towns themselves, that had been established to deal with an exploding gold-seeking population soon became unnecessary.

Building the Impossible Railway

Construction of a modern transportation system for the Yukon actually began during the gold rush, when many Klondikers started traveling the White Pass to get from the Pacific coast to the Yukon River, where they could then go by boat down to Dawson City and its nearby gold fields. The elevation of White Pass is only 2,917 feet (889 meters), so of all the routes from the coast to the interior of the Yukon, it had

■ A small settlement at the summit of White Pass in 1899.

the most gradual slope going over the mountains. For this reason, a group of entrepreneurs led by the Church brothers of London decided in 1898 that this was the best route for a railroad from Skagway to the new town of Whitehorse. They believed they could make a lot of money servicing the Klondike goldfields with a railway line.

When this group initially looked into the feasibility of building such a railroad, experts told them it was impossible. The project was simply beyond the engineering capabilities of the day. However, a Canadian contractor, Michael J. Heney, persuaded the group that in spite of the tremendous difficulties he could build the railway. Work started on the immense project that same year, 1898. Almost every mile of the route had to be blasted out with dynamite. Because of the steep grade—it was to be the steepest railway line in all of Canada—timber had to be imported from the south for railway ties and for the many bridges that needed to be built. Local timber was just too weak for the stress the tracks would have to bear as heavy trains pushed up and down the steep slope.

Speedy construction was considered vital to take advantage of the booming gold rush, so the crews building the railroad worked day and night in the summer months. But when

■ *The first train on the White Pass and Yukon Railway carries its first load of passengers.*

winter came, they were often driven out of White Pass completely by the snow and frequent blizzards. Nevertheless, by July 29, 1900, the crew working eastward from Skagway finally linked up near Carcross with the crew working in the opposite direction from Whitehorse.

By the time the 110-mile (177-kilometer) railway line was completed, it had cost $10 million—a considerable fortune in those days. But also by then, the gold rush was winding down. The Klondike miners were leaving in droves. So the prospects of the railway becoming a booming transportation business faded even before the first engine traveled down the shiny new tracks. The White Pass and Yukon Railway company struggled to stay afloat financially, carrying the small number of passengers and the little freight that still needed transport after the gold rush ended.

The construction and subsequent operation of the railway was accomplished without receiving any government funding. Yet the track, which ran over tremendously rugged terrain, still had to be maintained—an expensive proposition that often taxed the railway company to its limits. Trains frequently ran behind schedule, a fact that

■ Yukon's Czar

During the Klondike gold rush, George Jeckell came to the Yukon to teach school. But in 1913, his skills landed him the job of comptroller (chief accountant) for the territory. Money to run the Yukon's government came mainly from federal grants, taxes on liquor, fur exports, and hunting licenses. As the population declined, this funding dried up and civil servants were laid off. In 1932 the federal government combined Jeckell's position with that of the Gold Commissioner to make Jeckell the chief executive of the Yukon. (The title of comptroller was changed to controller in 1936; the federal government reestablished the office of the commissioner in 1947.)

Jeckell was often described as an unassuming man more comfortable following instructions—which in this case came from the federal government—than daring to find a new course. As more and more white people left the Yukon during the early years of the twentieth century, however, Jeckell emerged as the dominant administrative force in the region. He slowly added the offices of income tax inspector, mayor of Dawson (ex officio), public works agent, and registrar of land titles to his roster of duties. He soon found himself running the entire territory almost single-handedly, a job he held until his retirement as controller in 1946.

became the subject of jokes among Yukoners. Despite the economic hardships, the company managed to keep the trains running.

A Shadow of a Government

As residents left the Yukon, the federal government cut its subsidies to the region and thereby contributed to its ongoing economic woes. The legislative council in Dawson City, the territory's first capital, increasingly found itself powerless to do much. In 1918, the federal government even tried to abolish the legislative council. Yukoners protested and managed to save the council, though it was reduced to just three members. Federal officials did abolish as an unjustifiable expense the office of the commissioner—the "Gold Commissioner," who reported to the federal Minister of the Interior, was to be the territory's chief executive for the next fourteen years. Apart from the people who worked in the transportation and mining industries, the remaining nonnatives were mainly administrators, missionaries, or traders. By 1921, the territory's population hit a historic low of fewer than 4,000, and it hardly increased over the next two decades.

As the number of newcomers continued to decline in the 1930s, the Yukon government shrank until it eventually consisted, in effect, of just a single individual, controller George Jeckell. Historian William R. Morrison summarized the post-Klondike period when he wrote,

> The legacy of the 1890s for the Yukon was an infrastructure that, modern for its day, proceeded to decay over the next forty years; an economy dependent on world mineral prices; a white population that shrank in twenty years from 40,000 to 2,500 and did not begin to grow again until the Second World War. The wealth of the North had always left the North, extracted by outsiders, and this was as true of the gold of the Yukon as it was of the furs.[17]

First Nations Struggle to Adapt

The First Nations populations, on the other hand, having been mostly excluded from the riches associated with the gold rush, continued to follow the ways of life they had known for nearly a century, and so sidestepped modernization and the many changes it would bring. Native peoples lived off the land and supplemented this by making crafts and trading furs, which continued as a small but still viable economic activity.

Discriminatory hiring practices by European owners mostly prevented natives from working in the gold mines. But even if they could have been hired for these jobs, they probably would not have kept them for long. The natives were accustomed to a lifestyle of intermittent work that followed the seasons. So when they did take regular employment, it was usually something like cutting firewood for the steamboats on the Yukon River—jobs natives could do for a short time before returning to their communities. As they had done since their first contacts with white civilization, they took advantage of new economic opportunities only when it suited them.

During these years, the native population had a higher birthrate than in earlier years. But this was offset by a higher mortality rate from the diseases brought by whites, so their numbers appeared to remain unchanged. The exact First Nations population figures in the early twentieth century are not known, but historians estimate that the number was probably only 20 or 30 percent of the figure it had been a century before.

The overall economic picture was tenuous. The territory seemed to be in a permanent decline, with the white population largely dependent on one industry—mining.

Industrialized Gold Mining

After the gold rush, plenty of gold remained in the Yukon though it was no longer concentrated in high-yield deposits. Miners could not gather sufficient quantities of gold using the labor-intensive Klondike methods to make small-scale mining worthwhile. It now took expensive, more powerful equipment and facilities to make gold mining profitable, so it was mostly big companies—those with an ability to raise large sums of investment money—that still mined for gold.

After 1900, many individual miners sold their claims to such companies, or "concessions" (so-called because the companies had to make special arrangements with the federal government to obtain the right to mine large areas). Other Klondike miners left and simply let their claims lapse, in which case the companies often just moved in to take them over.

■ *A mining company uses high-pressure water cannons to blast away rock from a cliff face.*

A mining dredge extracts gold from a creek bed.

The first advance in mining methods was the introduction of hydraulic mining. This replaced the old approach of using fires to melt the top layer of frozen soil and gravel, which could then be stripped from the land and sifted for gold. These fires often burned out of control and as a result most of the forests surrounding Dawson City had been destroyed. Forests farther away were spared at least temporarily because the soil-melting technique was too inefficient for the smaller quantities of gold that now remained.

The technique of hydraulic mining that replaced soil-melting, however, was hardly any gentler on the environment. Miners used high-pressure water hoses, fed by water funneled out of local streams, to blast away at hillsides and stream banks. Soon, this method of mining was augmented with floating dredges that chewed up to 12 feet into the creek beds to extract the gold that lay there. Between the years of 1900 and 1914, over 75 percent of the $250 million in gold mined in the Yukon used these new mining techniques.

Soon after this, however, World War I sparked a world gold depression that lasted from 1917 to 1923. Gold mining in the Yukon came to a virtual stop, but then picked up again in 1924. The next five years saw gold production in the region reach its peak. Still, it was a volatile business, with production increasing when world gold markets were good and declining again in depression years. In 1964, the year when the last gold dredge ceased operation, large-scale gold mining in the Yukon ended for many years. Gold mining may not have been the stable industry many Yukoners hoped it would be, but it did serve to transform the region in other ways, not the least of which was spurring the development of the railway.

Mining Other Metals

With a railway in place, mining other Yukon ores became possible. Back in the gold rush days, miners had discovered a massive copper deposit around Whitehorse. However, low copper prices on the world market, coupled with the high cost of transporting the copper ore to the railroad once it was built, meant that efforts to exploit this discovery were slow and sporadic. For example, in 1906, copper prices suddenly soared, and a railway spur line was started toward the copper deposits. Copper prices then fell again, and work stopped on the spur line for three years.

It was not until World War I dramatically increased the demand for copper that copper mining in the Yukon became profitable and was pursued in earnest. In 1910, 286,000 pounds of copper were exported from the territory. This rose to over 1.8 million pounds in 1913 and eventually to 2.8 million pounds in 1916. However, the wartime boom did not last. High production costs, due to the need to constantly pump out water that seeped into the mines, coupled with high transportation costs, meant that when copper prices fell after the war, it was again no longer viable to mine the copper. The copper mines closed down in 1920, and then made a temporary comeback later in that decade. But it was not until 1960 that mining copper again became a significant part of the Yukon's economy.

Meanwhile, in 1919, silver-lead ore had been discovered on Keno Hill near Mayo. A concentrating mill, which partially extracted these metals from the ore, was built. By 1924, silver-lead production had exceeded the Klondike gold production. But when the ore ran out in the area in 1932, this too was closed down.

In 1953, a prospector discovered a large lead-zinc deposit 120 miles (190 kilometers) northeast of Whitehorse. In 1966, more extensive exploration of this area started, which resulted in sixteen thousand claims being staked. Three years later, the Cyprus Anvil Mining Company began full-scale mining at one of the largest open-pit mines of its type in the world. Cyprus Anvil also constructed the town of Faro nearby to provide housing and services for its workers. By 1978, the Cyprus Anvil Mine was Canada's leading producer of lead and was responsible for a major chunk of the Yukon's gross territorial product. Faro's population of 1,500 in 1991 made it the second-largest town in the territory.

The Cyprus Anvil Mine, and thus Faro has since experienced the ups and downs typical of Yukon mining. When mineral prices on the world market drop below a certain level, it is no longer profitable to mine Cyprus Anvil and the pit closes. This had occurred twice in the 1990s. Most recently, the mine closed in 1997. Faro's population—more than half of which depended on the mine for employment—plunged from 1,226 in 1997 to about 350 in late 1999.

This had been the continuing economic story of the Yukon for most of the past century. Changes in the economic health of the territory sprang from world events over which Yukoners had little control. Indeed, one of the key developments that transformed the face of the Yukon during the twentieth century was the direct result of a remote event—the Japanese bombing of Pearl Harbor on December 7, 1941, and America's immediate entry into World War II. Within a few weeks of these events, plans were drawn up to build a highway that would link Alaska, through Canada and the Yukon, to the contiguous United States.

Cutting a Highway Through the Wilderness

The highway, first called the Alcan Highway and then later the Alaska Highway, was considered vital by American military planners to provide a safe, alternate transportation route between Alaska and the American ports of the Pacific Northwest. It was feared that ships, which had been the lower states' only transportation link to Alaska, might become vulnerable to attack by Japanese submarines.

The idea of such a highway was not new. In fact, people in both the Yukon and Alaska had been campaigning for such a highway for over a decade. But neither the Canadian nor the American government had been willing to spend the money required to build it. In the panic of early 1942, however, all economic considerations were thrown aside. America believed that Alaska needed to be protected. And the Canadian

■ *The Alaska Highway stretches 1,500 miles from British Columbia to Alaska.*

government was not opposed to the idea of a highway, as long as Canada did not have to pay for it and the Americans agreed to turn control of it over to Canada after the war. The Canadians granted American engineers free rein over where to build the road and what materials to use.

Building the highway proved to be one of the most remarkable engineering feats ever completed in North America. The challenge lay both in its length—it would stretch more than 1,500 miles (2,400 kilometers) from Dawson Creek in British Columbia to Fairbanks, Alaska—and in the tough conditions in which it needed to be rapidly built. Many times during the construction, the difficulty of building on permafrost slowed progress. In one section near Beaver Creek, for example, a large expanse of permafrost turned into an ice-bottomed bog when the top layer of earth was scraped away.

Despite such difficulties, it was completed—at least to the point that heavy trucks could travel along it during the months it was frozen—in eight months during 1942 at a cost of almost $150 million. The tremendous speed of construction was accomplished through a massive mobilization of laborers and heavy equipment, including a large number of graders, tractors,

■ The Pitiful Pipeline

Concurrent with the work on the Alaska Highway, another large defense project was launched in the Yukon: the construction of the Canol ("Canadian oil") pipeline. The idea was to lay a 620-mile (1,000-kilometer) pipeline to ship oil from a small existing oil field at Norman Wells on the Mackenzie River (Northwest Territories) to a new refinery that would be built at Whitehorse. The Canol pipeline would assure a reliable supply of oil and fuel for American airfields in the Pacific Northwest and Alaska.

Unlike the magnificent achievement of the highway, however, this was a questionable endeavor right from the start. The concern that Japan might be able to disrupt the supply of oil to Alaska had begun to fade in mid-1943 by the time the U.S. Army Corps of Engineers started constructing the pipeline. Engineers also underestimated the difficulty of building a pipeline through the almost-unknown frozen mountains and mosquito-infested valleys of east-central Yukon. Some 25,000 laborers (including about 150 women) did manage to finish the pipeline in February 1944. It operated only for about a year, however, before the Whitehorse refinery was shut down.

In his account of building the pipeline, B.C. Barry wrote, "Today, to be sure, it is not easy to take Canol seriously. Its 4- and 6-inch pipeline, puny by our standards, was puny by the standards of the 1940s as well. Moreover, some of Canol's technology was the crudest to be found in the modern repertoire: the wood stove, the pack horse, and the dog sled . . . it often proceeded like a situation comedy, as when the Mackenzie River mud swallowed whole vehicles, or a workman drove a truck through a mess hall after a lunch he did not like."

Late in the war, a U.S. Senate committee headed by Senator Harry Truman investigated wasted military spending, and the Canol pipeline became one of the committee's key examples. (It cost more than five times the initial estimate of $24 million.) The project became an embarrassment to the American government, and in 1947 the pipeline was dismantled. Its memory lingers in the form of the Canol Road, from the Alaska Highway to the Yukon/Northwest Territories border, and the Canol Heritage Trail, a hiking trail, from there to Norman Wells.

■ *A section of the 620-mile Canol pipeline.*

and dump trucks. Altogether, nearly forty thousand men and women worked on the highway and on other associated defense projects—three times the combined population of the Yukon and the Northwest Territories at the time.

First Nations Ambivalent Toward Highway

Construction of the Alaska Highway had various effects on First Nations peoples. The immediate effect in a number of instances was negative. The men who built the highway shot multitudes of animals, fished the streams to depletion, and polluted the water. These were natural resources upon which the natives still depended. In addition, many of the native people were not even told that the highway was being built. In a few cases, they found out about it only when bulldozers came crashing out of the bush and into their communities.

Highway construction also led to increased disease rates among First Nations peoples. In the winter of 1942–1943, epidemics of measles, pneumonia, and influenza killed numerous native children and elderly. The increased disease rates were due at least in part to how quickly outsiders who were still infectious could reach remote areas. The highway project meant that people could now reach tribal lands in a matter of days or hours instead of weeks.

Modern Links

As unfortunate as all this was for native peoples, the Alaska Highway and the Canol pipeline nevertheless served to transform the Yukon in a number of positive ways. Along with other defense-related projects, they linked the Yukon more closely to both Canada and the United States. Until the war, the Yukon did not even have phone service—it had relied on telegraph and radio telephones for communication to the outside world. Many other facilities were also constructed to go along with the highway, from airfields to housing. All this construction had an immediate impact on the Yukon economy. The influx of so many people working on these projects created new towns and turned small communities like Whitehorse into boomtowns.

The men actually building the highway and other facilities lived in tent communities that moved as the construction moved. But thousands of support staff moved into the local communities, altering them completely. In 1941, for example, the summer population of Whitehorse was about eight

■ A History of Environmental Upheaval

Newcomers to the Yukon, through their efforts to survive economically, often have had a devastating impact on the Yukon environment. Although they came at different times for different purposes, the outcome was largely the same. For example, during the height of the fur trade, the natives' limited culling of fur-bearing animals gave way to wholesale slaughter as companies competed for higher and higher profits.

When the first gold prospectors arrived in the area surrounding Dawson in the late 1800s, they cut down and burned most of the trees in the area to melt the frozen ground for panning. In a later mining method, high-pressure hoses raked riverbeds and banks, causing devastating damage. Even more dramatically, the huge dredging machines of the 1920s and 1930s ripped large quantities of gravel from riverbeds and deposited great mounds of residue across the landscape.

In 1943, during the construction of the Canol pipeline, many of the men working on the project were grossly inexperienced. Poor workmanship led to many cracks and breaks along the pipeline. It leaked fuel that soaked into the ground and spilled into the lakes and streams, causing long-term adverse effects on the local populations of migratory birds, beavers, and muskrats. Abandoned vehicles and machinery also litter the pipeline route to this day.

Men working on the Alaska Highway and on the Canol pipeline were also inclined to burn peat or mosses just to keep the mosquitoes away. These fires would sometimes flare out of control because of petroleum spills and high winds, leading to raging forest fires.

■ *Deforestation is one of the environmental problems that the Yukon has faced throughout its history.*

■ *The Mile "0" marker of the Alaska Highway in Dawson Creek, British Columbia.*

hundred people. In winter months, it was even less. Yet by 1943, Whitehorse was home to more than ten thousand people, four-fifths of them Americans. This affected every facet of life in the town, even entertainment. A movie theater was built, as were numerous baseball diamonds. In fact, the Americans' love of baseball is said to have resulted in White-horse having more baseball diamonds per capita than any other postwar North American city.

Of all the developments, however, the Alaska Highway was the one that had the most lasting impact on the territory. Once the initial road was finished, it was widened and improved. The Canadian government took over the 1,250-mile (2,000-kilometer) Canadian section of the highway in 1946,

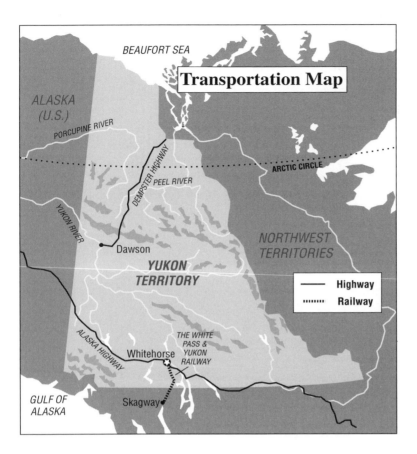

and has since turned over local control to the provincial and territorial governments of British Columbia and the Yukon respectively. Canada paid the United States $108 million for buildings, telephone systems, and other assets constructed by the Americans. But as was originally agreed, it paid nothing for the highway itself.

Today, the highway serves as a major transportation link for the majority of Yukon communities. To celebrate the highway's fiftieth birthday in 1992, paving of its entire length was finally finished. Maintaining the Yukon portion costs the territorial government $40 million a year—winter thaws produce massive potholes, and summer rainstorms can lead to extensive washouts.

An Economic Stimulant

Despite the high cost of maintenance, the Alaska Highway has continued to stimulate the Yukon economy. Tourism, for example, blossomed along the road, and the motels, gas stations, and restaurants that opened to serve tourists brought much-needed income to many communities. The highway also greatly contributed to the growth and development of White-horse, which not only became the Yukon's largest community but also eventually replaced Dawson as the Yukon's capital in 1953.

Today, it is hard to imagine what life in the Yukon would be like if the events, from the Klondike gold rush to the building of the Alaska Highway, had not brought a flood of outsiders. The people who ultimately benefited, however, were not the people who came to build, but those who stayed—those who were determined to make real Yukon communities they could call home.

Daily Life, Arts, and Culture

As remote as Yukon is, the lives its citizens lead are similar in many ways to those of other Canadians. Yukoners today watch many of the same television programs (beamed in by satellite) and movies that other Canadians do, read similar books and magazines, and listen to the same CDs—though added shipping costs mean Yukoners often have to pay more for these items. Territory residents work in gas stations and government offices, and go to churches and schools, just like folks south and east.

It is also true, however, that even with a total population that is smaller than, for example, at least thirty cities and towns in Ontario, the Yukon has managed to develop a unique culture that reflects its heritage. It has produced or inspired writers and artists of world renown. And it continues to draw newcomers, year in and year out, just as it did during its gold rush days more than a century ago. Except today, the riches that visitors take away with them glitter in intangible ways, especially as memories of a wild and still largely untamed land.

Where the Jobs Are

Although the mining industry remains a major economic force within the Yukon, it seldom directly employs more than one thousand residents. A much higher percentage of Yukoners are employed by the federal, territorial, or municipal governments—about forty-five hundred in all. The majority of

■ Buildings such as this old store in Dawson City have been restored from the days of the gold rush.

these work for the territorial government. The nontourism related service and construction sectors employ another twenty-five hundred workers.

Tourism is a major employer, providing about thirty-five hundred jobs. Yukon's tourism industry is concentrated during the short summer season. The majority of visitors arrive either to enjoy the magnificent national parks or to see the ghost towns and abandoned mines of the Klondike region. Many historic buildings in Dawson have been restored or reconstructed, and gold rush relics are on display throughout the town. Visitors are still intrigued by stories of Yukon's wild Klondike days, when fortunes were made—and often lost—overnight. Much of this tourist industry consists of small businesses employing shopkeepers, clerks, and guides. When tourists leave at the end of the summer, many of these businesses virtually close down and simply prepare for the flood of tourists next year.

Today, the fur industry is a minor segment of the economy that has not changed all that much from how it was operated a century ago. It is mainly First Nations people who continue to trap animals such as beaver, marten, and wolverines and process the pelts. Animal rights concerns and other factors have caused a decline in the demand for fur in recent years.

Health and Education

Providing social services such as health and education is a major challenge for the territory. One obvious difficulty relates to how large and sparsely populated the Yukon is. No matter how remote, small communities still need to have health facilities for all residents, and schools for all children from kindergarten to grade twelve. Providing services is expensive but the Yukon government has made a major commitment to health and education.

Although the Yukon has only two hospitals, with a total of seventy-four staffed beds, it has nine additional health treatment centers in the more remote communities. As in other provinces and territories, most medical services in the Yukon are covered by a government-funded program. When medical emergencies arise in remote communities that cannot be handled at a local treatment center, patients will usually be flown to one of the hospitals.

The Yukon also has twenty-eight public schools, attended by about fifty-eight hundred students. The one college, Yukon College, has a main campus in Whitehorse and a dozen smaller campuses in communities throughout the region. The college has an enrollment of less than nine hundred full-time and fifty-two hundred part-time students. It offers only the first two years of university-level education. Students have to go outside the territory to continue their college education, although now that students can also take courses over the Internet, this is starting to change.

The Yukon is able to provide social services in part only because of the support it receives from the federal government. Up to 70 percent of the territory's annual revenues come from transfer payments made by the federal government to the territorial government. Without these transfer payments, the Yukon would have to reduce its support of education, medical services, and highway maintenance.

A Lively Arts Scene

The Yukon's remoteness has encouraged a creative and open culture that is rich in art and in cultural events. Indeed, given how few people actually live in the area, it is quite remarkable how much actually goes on in the territory throughout the year. The Yukon offers a year-round smorgasbord of theater groups, singers, dancers, musicians, storytellers, and concert groups. Much of this activity occurs in Whitehorse, with one of the most popular venues being the new Yukon Arts Centre,

■ *The Gold Rush Inn Motel in the capital city of Whitehorse, where most of the Yukon's cultural life is concentrated.*

the territory's largest performance and visual arts facility. Entertainers also perform on stages at Yukon College and at other locations in the city. Many of these entertainers also travel to other Yukon communities, usually performing in local schools.

Whitehorse is also home to a number of museums. The MacBride Museum of the Yukon displays much of the history of the territory including First Nations culture, the Klondike gold stampede, the Northwest Mounted Police (merged with the Dominion Police in 1919 to become the Royal Canadian Mounted Police), and even the postal service. One display, for example, features an old sod-covered log cabin that was once the post office. The museum also exhibits the world's largest public collection of Yukon gold.

The Old Log Church Museum in Whitehorse is interesting both as a building and for its contents. It is one of the oldest buildings in Whitehorse, having been constructed as an Anglican church in 1901 to replace the tent where church services were being held. Although most of Whitehorse's buildings from this period no longer stand, the log church has been fully restored. The museum houses exhibits from native cultures, early European explorations, the gold rush, and missionary history.

In the summer, the longest running theatrical production in Whitehorse is the Frantic Follies, an 1890s vaudeville show

■ Vibrant Whitehorse

About 70 percent of the Yukon's residents live in the capital city of Whitehorse. The crescent-shaped city spreads out on a level shelf on the west bank of the Yukon River, its back sheltered by two hundred-foot-high mountain escarpments. Because it is in the southern part of the Yukon, temperatures are more moderate compared to towns farther north, such as Dawson and Mayo. In July, the average temperature is 57° F (14°C), and the average January temperature is 0°F (–18°C).

In spite of its remote location, Whitehorse is a vibrant and diverse community. It has two newspapers, one television station, and three radio stations. The city is small enough that downtown stores, restaurants, and hotels are within walking distance of each other. Many tourists visit Whitehorse during the summer months for its cultural and entertainment attractions, ranging from the MacBride Museum to the S.S. *Klondike*. The latter is a beached sternwheeler riverboat that was built in 1937, retired in 1955, and recently restored as a museum to its former glory.

Whitehorse also hosts a number of annual events. The weeklong Yukon Sourdough Rendezvous festival has been a Whitehorse staple each February since it was started by the American military during World War II to celebrate the end of winter. Almost all of the city's residents take part, with many dressing up in turn-of-the-century costumes. Stores and restaurants are decorated in a gold rush theme, and the festival features dances, concerts, and an air show as well as a string of offbeat events such as a beard-growing contest and a fiddling competition. These attract people from all over the Yukon as well as from outside the territory.

■ *A renovated sternwheeler riverboat, the S.S.* Klondike, *is one of Whitehorse's most popular attractions.*

put on every night at the Westmark Whitehorse Hotel. The Follies features dances, comedy skits, and songs based on the Klondike theme. Local saloons and Whitehorse theaters also present gold rush acts. Many of these events are geared for the tourists who stop in Whitehorse as part of a Yukon experience that must also include the territory's "second city"—Dawson.

Dynamic Dawson

Canada has designated numerous historic sites in Dawson, helping the town to attract some sixty thousand tourists every summer to witness and take part in a variety of gold rush–related events. Ever since gold was discovered on August 17, 1896, in a nearby tributary of the Klondike River, Dawson has celebrated the Discovery Days Festival on the weekend closest to August 17. Events include a parade, dances, raft and canoe races, and fruit and flower shows, all of which have maintained the same character since 1900.

Another of the territory's most popular cultural events is the Dawson City Music Festival. Each July, it brings musicians from all over the continent to play folk, rock, jazz, blues, world beat, and traditional music under the midnight

■ Diamond Tooth Gertie's Gambling Hall

Canada's first, and for a long time, only, legal casino, Diamond Tooth Gertie's, has a history that goes back to the gold rush days. Klondike dance halls of the time were raucous places but they offered a refined attraction: dance-hall girls. These were not the high-kicking, petticoat-showing dance-hall girls popular in cities such as Paris. The Klondikers preferred waltzes, polkas, and reels, and the women showed nothing more daring than an exposed ankle. At the height of the gold rush, the Yukon dance-hall girls would charge as much as $5 a waltz, and the lonely miners would pay that much just for a dance.

These girls often used nicknames, and one of the most famous was Diamond Tooth Gertie, whose real name was Gertie Lovejoy. Her dance-hall nickname was given to her because she wore a small diamond between her two front teeth. The popular Dawson casino named after her retains much of the earthy atmosphere of her era. Today, from May to September, tourists and gamblers alike still fill the hall at Diamond Tooth Gertie's to play roulette, blackjack, or poker. Slot machines line the walls and nightly shows feature can can girls and a Diamond Tooth Gertie impersonator.

sun. Dawson also hosts the highlight of the Yukon social scene: the formal Commissioner's Ball held each summer at the Palace Grand Theatre which was built in 1899 by gold rush entrepreneur Arizona Charlie Meadows and recently restored. It is not often that the people of Dawson get to dress up.

Some of the profits from Diamond Tooth Gertie's Gambling Hall help to restore other historic town buildings, which include the 1901 Old Post Office and the 1912 Commissioner's Residence. Strolling through downtown Dawson on its wooden walkways is truly a step back in time.

■ *A street in Dawson, July 1992, the Yukon's "second city."*

Small-Town Life

Many of the Yukon's smaller communities also have their own unique cultural and sporting events. For example, Burwash Landing, on the Alaska Highway at the northwestern shore of Kluane Lake, has a population of scarcely more than one hundred. Yet it is home to the "Burwash 27" Ice Races, a car race on frozen Kluane Lake in mid-April with $10,000 in prizes.

Most of the residents of the Yukon's remote communities must be content to eke out a livelihood in this rugged land, surviving one way or another as best they can. The flavor of

■ Dogsledding, Yesterday and Today

Long before the arrival of Europeans, Yukon natives were depending upon dogsleds for transportation much of the year. The early sleds were like toboggans with a flat bottom. Europeans settlers to the Yukon also quickly came to appreciate the advantage of this form of transportation. The Europeans tweaked the design to build the large, basket-shaped carriers on two narrow runners that are still used today.

A dogsled team usually consists of two to twelve animals, although five large malamutes (also known as huskies) made up the preferred Northwest Mounted Police dog team of the early 1900s. This is because of malamutes' stamina and their tough feet, which must endure exposure to rough snow and ice. Originally, French-speaking sled drivers shouted the command "Marché!" to their dogs. The English heard this command as "Mush," and it soon caught on as the customary signal for "Go" to the dog team.

Today, dogsleds have been replaced by high-powered snowmobiles for everyday transportation, but the dogsledding tradition lives on in various races held each year. The toughest dogsled race in the world runs for 1,000 miles (1,600 kilometers) between Fairbanks, Alaska, and Whitehorse. It is called the Yukon Quest, and "mushers" come from all over the world to compete for the $30,000 first prize, even though this race is especially arduous and even dangerous.

Depending on the weather, the race lasts from ten to twenty days, with a compulsory thirty-six-hour layover in Dawson. This layover is the only ex-

this struggle has been captured by numerous writers, including one of the most famous writers of the early twentieth century.

Jack London

Jack London was born in 1876 in San Francisco. His parents were poor and his formal education was sporadic, including two years of high school and one semester at the University of California. At seventeen, he signed on with a sailing vessel bound for Japan and then the Bering Sea. In 1898 he joined the throngs rushing into the Klondike in search of gold. His brief experiences there provided inspiration for far-north adventure stories still read today for their realistic, sometimes autobiographical, depictions of bravery, hardship, and despair.

Among London's most popular books is *The Call of the Wild*, published in 1903. In this tale about a dog that takes up with a wolf pack, London said of the untamed Yukon, "No lazy,

tended rest for mushers and dogs. The sleds must carry all the mushers' and dogs' food and supplies needed for the trip. Dogs are not allowed to be added or replaced in a team once the race starts, and the teams can receive no outside help during the race, save from other contestants.

■ *A team of huskies pulls a sled. Dogsledding is one of the Yukon's oldest forms of transportation.*

sun-kissed life was this, with nothing to do but loaf and be bored. Here was neither peace, nor rest, nor a moment's safety. All was confusion and action, and every moment life and limb were in peril."[18]

London was an adventurer who never settled in the Yukon—or really anywhere else—but preferred the hard-drinking lifestyle of the war correspondent and world traveler. Financial difficulties and other problems drove him to commit suicide at the age of forty, but a number of his popular Yukon-based works, such as *White Fang*, remain in print and have been made into popular films.

The Poet of the Yukon

Like Jack London, Robert Service is often identified as a "Yukon writer" although he was born elsewhere and spent only a part of his life living in the Yukon. It was during Service's time in the Yukon, however, that he penned such Canadian classics as "The

■ *Writer Jack London poses in a wide-brimmed hat and knee-high rubber boots.*

Cremation of Sam McGee," "The Shooting of Dan McGrew," and "The Law of the Yukon."

Service was born in England in 1874 and emigrated to Canada as a twenty-year-old. He traveled in California and British Columbia before becoming a bank clerk in the early 1900s for the Canadian Bank of Commerce in Whitehorse, and later Dawson City, in the newly formed Yukon Territory. His job was to weigh gold dust and keep the ledger books. His imagination was inspired by the people, and the wealth and the greed that he saw, and he began writing his haunting phrases about the lure of Yukon gold. Yukoners enjoyed hearing his lyrics, but to them he remained the shy young banker and "the solitary walker"[19] who lived across the way.

After writing his first set of poems, which he called *Songs of a Sourdough*, he decided that he might try to publish them. Service sent his work to an eastern publisher, along with a check to cover the publishing costs. He was completely astonished when the check was sent back to him with a note saying the publisher would cover the costs. Soon after the publication of Service's first poems in 1907, they were being recited in parks, workplaces, and dinner parties throughout the United States and Canada.

In the summer of 1909, for the first time the governor general of Canada, Albert Grey, was making a visit to the Yukon. Dawson City was buzzing with excitement awaiting his arrival. When Grey arrived in August, his first words to the commissioner were, "Does Robert Service live far from here? I would like to meet him." The people of Dawson were amazed that a man of Grey's importance would have an interest in their modest bank clerk. Yukoners, including Service himself, had been totally unaware of the fame that had grown around his poetry.

Service eventually left the territory and returned to England. He drove an ambulance during World War I and traveled widely until his death in France in 1958. Although he wrote many poems and novels based on his experiences in Europe and elsewhere, he is still best remembered as Canada's "poet of the Yukon," and a cabin where Service lived in Dawson is still preserved for tourists to see.

A Modern Voice of the Yukon

Canadian author Pierre Berton and his mother, Laura Berton, also an author, are two other famous Yukon cultural exports. Laura, a Dawson City schoolteacher, wrote of her experiences in the territory in *I Married the Yukon*. Pierre, now one

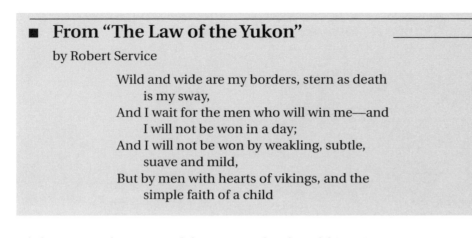

From "The Law of the Yukon"

by Robert Service

> Wild and wide are my borders, stern as death
>   is my sway,
> And I wait for the men who will win me—and
>   I will not be won in a day;
> And I will not be won by weakling, subtle,
>   suave and mild,
> But by men with hearts of vikings, and the
>   simple faith of a child

of the country's most widely respected cultural historians, was raised in Dawson. He is the author of dozens of books about Canada, including *The Klondike Fever* and *The Klondike Quest*.

> As Berton has noted, It has often been said (usually by Americans) that there is no great difference between those who live south of the forty-ninth parallel and those who live on the Canadian side; but the Klondike experience supplies a good deal of evidence to support the theory that our history and our geography have helped to make us a distinct people—not better and not worse—but different in style, background, attitude, and temperament from our neighbours.[20]

Native Writers

While most of the best-known writers in Yukon are European in background, the native populations of Yukon also share in the literary traditions. Angela Sidney, who died in 1991, was one of the last speakers and teachers of the Tagish language. She recorded and published the songs, stories, and traditions of her people in books such as *Life Lived Like a Story* and *My Stories Are My Wealth*.

Edith Josie from Old Crow is another example of a talented native writer who established a solid following in the Yukon, if not nationally. The First Nations community of Old Crow, located south of the Vuntut National Park in northern Yukon, is the only settlement in the Yukon with no road connections. With fewer than three hundred residents and lying 75 miles (120 kilometers) north of the Arctic Circle, everything from outside comes into Old Crow by air. Nevertheless, for years, Old Crow elder Edith Josie's

■ Sourtoe Cocktail, Anyone?

During the Klondike gold rush, there was so much gold circulating that gold dust and flakes often fell between the floorboards of many of the saloons and residences. These days it is not uncommon for a Yukoner to lift up a board or two in hopes of coming up with a little treasure. In 1973, riverboat captain Dick Stevenson, on his way to Dawson, stopped off at an abandoned cabin near Sixty-Mile River. Lifting a floorboard to look for gold, he was surprised to find a petrified human toe!

When Stevenson arrived in Dawson, he went straight to a saloon and began showing off his petrified prize. Tired of hearing his story, a fellow drinker suggested that if Stevenson were man enough, he would put the toe in his drink and take a swallow. Stevenson, being the devil-may-care Yukoner that he was, could not resist a dare. A newspaper reporter witnessed the act and a Dawson City tradition was born.

Stevenson's strange practice lives on at the Sourtoe Cocktail Club at Dawson's Downtown Hotel. Anyone with nerve enough can, for a small fee, order a drink (it doesn't have to be alcoholic) into which is placed a dehydrated and salt-preserved human toe. To receive a certificate as a "sourtoer," one has to allow the toe to touch one's lips while drinking the "sourtoe cocktail." Actually swallowing the toe, however, is not suggested.

■ *Early miners weigh gold dust at a Yukon saloon.*

columns, called "Here Are the News," were published regularly in the *Whitehorse Star* and in many other newspapers. They brought those from the south glimpses of a unique northern lifestyle and its arts.

Each July, Whitehorse hosts the Yukon International Storytelling Festival, which has grown enormously since its humble beginnings in 1988. Most, though not all, of its participants come from countries of the circumpolar regions. Thus it attracts native and nonnative storytellers from all over northern Canada as well as participants from as far away as Greenland, Iceland, and Finland. Thousands attend the festival to hear the spellbinding tales of fact, fantasy, and legend. Participating native storytellers have included P.J. Johnson, Louise Profeit-LeBlanc, and Angela Sidney, all well known for helping to preserve and promote native culture in the territory.

Art and Handicrafts

The rugged yet beautiful landscape of the Yukon makes a dramatic subject not only for writers but also for visual artists. Ted Harrison, originally a schoolteacher, came to the Yukon in 1968 and painted what he saw. His brilliantly colored and deftly stylized scenes of the great landscapes to be found in the north have brought him national acclaim.

Sculptor Lilias Farley is another well-respected Yukon artist. She came for a short visit to see her brother in Whitehorse during 1948 and ended up staying until her death in 1989. Her wood and stone sculptures are famous for their clean, strong lines. Today her work is found in galleries in Vancouver and New York as well as in many private collections.

Perhaps the most notable art in the region comes from the native tradition. Due to their nomadic lifestyle, the First Nations people had no use for heavy items and permanent houses. As a result, much of their creative effort went into clothing such as moosehide moccasins, mukluks (boots), and mitts (mittens). The best jackets are soft, warm, and beautifully decorated with beads, leather, fur, and embroidery. Such work is still among the finest in the world. Traditional designs on these clothes, and on wooden carvings and paintings on houses, are often based on the emblems of the artist's mother's family. As Mark Zuehlke notes, "Contemporary Yukon First Nations people's arts traditions derive from historical patterns and methods of decorating clothing and other personal, ceremonial, and kinship-related objects." [21]

Mask carving and animal spirit–carving is being revived in southern Yukon with modern methods, breathing new life into the ancient art forms. Such native art is becoming more popular and commercially successful today. Moosehair tufting, for instance, the painstaking art of transforming small clumps of carefully trimmed moose or caribou hair into pictures, is increasingly in demand. Many Yukon shops now also carry small carvings, moosehorn jewelry, and other First Nations' handicrafts. The Society of Yukon Artists of Native Ancestry, located in Whitehorse, promotes and supports many of these artists and regularly sponsors exhibits of their work throughout the Yukon.

Rich Traditions Continue

Today the Yukon remains a vast wilderness, largely unsettled, with relatively few year-round residents. Economic concerns often cast a shadow over everyday life in the territory. Simply securing and paying for all the trappings of modern civilization, things that most people take for granted, continues to be a challenge—just as it has been a challenge in the Yukon for past centuries.

Unique Challenges Continue

Throughout the modern history of the Yukon, the region has been plagued by a fragile and uncertain economy. The region's financial uncertainties remain troublesome—the area still depends upon the vagaries of local supply of, and world demand for, natural resources, whether gold or lumber. Developing a more diversified economy is a major territorial goal for the new century, as is dealing in a fair manner with native land claims.

Where Mining Is King

Gold mining was the fuel for Yukon's first economic boom and the territory's reliance on mining has continued into current times. Gold, however, has long since been replaced by metals such as zinc and lead as the chief mineral products. Low world prices for gold, and the expense of extracting it from ore, virtually wiped out gold mining in Yukon during much of the twentieth century. In recent years, however, prices have been stable enough to inspire prospectors to stake out fresh claims along thousands of miles of creek beds.

After the Klondike gold rush, most gold mining was done by large companies capable of funding conventional "hard-rock" mining operations. Only one such hard-rock gold mine exists in the Yukon today, with all the others being placer gold operations. Placer gold is the small flakes and nuggets that can be sifted from creek beds and riverbanks. These new gold

■ *A Yukon miner drills for precious metals and minerals in a commercial mine.*

mines have generally been worked as sole enterprises or small family businesses by the claim holders, much as they were in the late 1890s. One difference is that modern technology allows for the use of small, cheap hydraulic systems and sluicing machines, usually powered by gasoline engines. Since 1980, annual placer gold production has ranged from 75,000 ounces (2,333 kilograms) to 160,000 ounces (4,977 kilograms). In 1999, 171 placer mines—"the family farm of the north"—produced 93,000 ounces (2,893 kilograms) of gold. Since the price of gold was about $320 per ounce, total placer production was valued at almost $30 million. This figure, however, represents a relatively small fraction of Yukon's total billion-dollar-per-year economy. Price fluctuations for metals other than gold have had a similar effect on the Yukon's other mining operations. As author Mark Zuehlke notes,

> When the Anvil Range mine at Faro is in operation, zinc is usually the dominant mineral being extracted in the territory. In 1996, for example, when the Anvil Range mine was open for most of the year, zinc production totaled $202 million. The previous year, however, when the mine was closed, production of zinc was a little less than $60 million. Lead and silver, the other two minerals that most contribute to the territory's economy, tend to be hit with the same downturns and upswings that influence the operation of the Faro mine. Despite the uncertainty that is endemic in mining operations throughout the world, the Yukon economy continues by necessity to depend on this industry for its economic fortune.[22]

Diversify or Die

Of the Yukon's total population, about fifteen thousand residents are counted among the labor force by the territorial government. About thirteen thousand of these are employed at any given time, and the remaining 13 percent are unemployed. This means that the Yukon has a relatively high unemployment rate compared to most other parts of Canada.

It is clear that part of the challenge for today's Yukon government is economic diversification. Other natural resources, however, do not seem to offer much reason for optimism. Agriculture is limited due to a short growing season, lack of arable land, and the long distance to potential markets. Likewise, although the forestry industry is important for local building and some furniture manufacturing, it has never really developed as an economic engine, again due to the distance to markets. (Moreover, unlike in other areas of Canada, the federal government, not the territorial one, manages the Yukon's forest resources.)

Unfortunately for the Yukon, even industries such as tourism, which is basically limited to the summer season, are affected by the territory's climate and location. "The territory's isolation and harsh northern climate," comments Zuehlke, "mean that non-resource-based manufacturing industries are virtually impossible to attract in numbers that might lead to a reduction of dependence on resource extraction industries."[23]

The Yukon government today recognizes the need to promote a more diversified economy and talks prominently about diversification in publications and Web pages. Oil exploration and hydroelectric development are being considered, though

■ Feeding the Boom in Tourism

In recent years up to 300,000 tourists have come to the Yukon. More than 80 percent of these visitors are from the United States. During the high point of the tourist season, there are far more tourists in the Yukon than residents. The numbers have generally been increasing by 1 to 3 percent each year.

Two main attractions draw these tourists to the Yukon: the magnificent wildernesses found in such places as the Yukon's Kluane National Park, and the Klondike Gold Rush attractions, especially around Dawson. There have been efforts to get more tourists coming in the winter months to enjoy winter sports there. However, as yet, winter visitors to the Yukon are still a small fraction of the numbers coming in the summer months.

■ *A group of campers enjoys the peace and solitude of Hoge Creek Pass in the Yukon's Kluane National Park.*

both are accompanied by environmental concerns. Another major project being considered is a natural gas pipeline that would follow the Alaska Highway. (Two gas wells in Yukon are among the top-producing wells in Canada, and the Canadian government recently transferred control of the territory's oil and gas resources to the territorial government.) Most Yukoners agree that a more stable economy for the territory will come only when it is not so dependent upon a few key industries.

■ A Young—and Dwindling—Population

The Yukon's population is young but it is also falling. The total population of the Yukon according to the 2001 census was fewer than twenty-nine thousand people. The huge territory includes only one city, three towns, four villages, two hamlets, thirteen unincorporated communities, and eight rural communities. The median age is thirty-five and only about 5 percent of the population is older than sixty-five. The Yukon Territory actually lost population from 1996 to 2001. The number of people who left the area or died was greater (by some two thousand individuals) than the number who moved into or were born in the territory. This is certainly a troubling trend for a place that is already so sparsely populated—if the net outflow continued at this rate, around the year 2070 the Yukon Territory will have no people left at all!

Late-Blooming Democracy

As a territory of Canada, the Yukon has had an unusual political history. Initially under the control of the Hudson's Bay Company, the territory was run by a commissioner and a six-member legislative council appointed by federal officials in the national capital of Ottawa from 1898 to 1902. For the next seven years the legislative council was increased in size to ten, half of whom were elected locally. Since 1909 the legislative councils (now called the Legislative Assembly), ranging in size from three to seventeen members, have been elected locally. The territory gained further power in 1970 when the federal government allowed the Yukon commissioner to establish a five-member (two elected) executive committee, now called the Executive Council. This council acts much like a provincial cabinet, administering department branches such as Education, Health and Social Services, and Energy, Mines, and Resources. In 1979, the federally appointed commissioner's role was reduced in favor of an elected government leader (now premier) in charge of the Executive Council.

Today, the six-member Executive Council is drawn from the elected political party that captures the most seats in the Legislative Assembly. In the general election held in April 2000, the people of the Yukon elected Yukon Liberal Party leader Patricia Duncan as premier. Elections for the legislature are held at least once every four years, although the party in power can call an election sooner if it feels it is appropriate. The territorial government has slowly been acquiring more of the powers most provinces have, including control over issues such as inland fisheries and mine safety. The Yukon is negotiating with the federal government for more control over water resources, forestry, native land claims, and health care.

The Yukon's political landscape is further complicated by the fact that the First Nations people of the Yukon never abandoned what they believed were their rights as "first owners" of the territory, and they eventually secured limited rights of self-government.

Losing Land

Until the 1950s, the Yukon's First Nations continued to have a relatively free hand to use most of the vast stretches of the Yukon, much as they always had. But the economic and industrial expansion of the 1950s, combined with the growing interest of the Canadian federal government in northern resources, resulted in the first real efforts to integrate the Yukon's First Nations people into the larger white society.

Land tenure and ownership issues were raised by the government. The licensing of big-game hunting and the registering of trap lines was initiated. Non–First Nations interests were granted huge oil and gas leases in northern Yukon areas, and hundreds of new claims were staked, not just around the areas where whites lived, but throughout the territory. Land near towns and along lakeshores was deeded to white ownership. For the first time, the First Nations people were separated from the land they had controlled for generations, and in a number of places they were told they must stop hunting on and using land that had not been legally assigned for their use.

Unlearning Native Culture

The Canadian government also began to urge First Nations peoples to move out of the bush into permanent communities, in part, so that youngsters could go to school. But for natives used to a seminomadic lifestyle, making the transition to life on a government reservation proved difficult. Government-funded welfare often seemed to increase social problems, such as alcoholism, while failing to reduce poverty or to improve educational achievement. In addition, poor housing and inadequate health care on the reservations added to the serious problems the First Nations people faced.

These problems were greatly increased by the system of boarding schools the Canadian government established for native children early in the twentieth century. Children were taken from their villages to be enrolled in distant boarding

schools for nine months of the year. More often than not, children starting at such schools spoke only their native language. But for integration purposes, authorities felt that fluency in English or French was vital. The boarding schools often forbade students from speaking their native tongues, with infractions sometimes leading to physical punishment.

    Because of the cost of transportation, some students did not even return home in the summer and spent six years or more at the school. When they did finally return home, they were strangers to their own families and communities. They lacked the traditional skills they needed to become functioning members of the native community. Yet they did not really fit in with white society either, and the alienation often led to alcoholism, violence, and despair. As the noted Yukon historians Ken Coates and William Morrison have noted:

    The economic and social turmoil of the post-war period struck at the very heart of Indian culture. Pulled into highway communities, forced into a culturally insensitive

■ *Canadian Indian children make their beds in a boarding school dormitory.*

education system, and encouraged to adapt to an economic system that offered few prospects, Yukon Indians sank into despair, a dislocated and colonized people. Whites reacted often with disapproval, occasionally with concern, to the visible signs of that despair—the startlingly impoverished villages, drunken people on the streets of Whitehorse, Indians outside grocery stores discounting their welfare chits for cash, and a surfeit of Indian names on the court docket—but were slow to appreciate the deep cultural loss that had attended the collapse of the harvesting economy and the far-reaching effects of the modernization of the Yukon.[24]

In recent years the territorial and federal governments have begun to try to make amends by funding special programs and offering loans, advice, supervision, and training for First Nations entrepreneurs. Tribes have also become more self-governing, although their lack of bureaucratic skills and political connections compared to those of government agents has prevented a significant shift in power.

The Rise of the Yukon Native Brotherhood

It fell to the First Nations peoples themselves to address their social conditions. In the mid-1960s, native leaders, led by the eloquent Elijah Smith, began forming a territory-wide organization known as the Yukon Native Brotherhood to end the "welfare thinking of Indian Affairs and our people,"[25] as Smith put it.

■ Creating Written Languages

Before Europeans came to the Yukon, the First Nations peoples there had no written language. In recent years, however, in an effort to ensure that the Yukon's traditional languages were preserved, work has been undertaken to create a written form of both the Athapaskan and Tlingit languages. The Yukon Native Language Center in Whitehorse has published both dictionaries and reading books in these two languages. The center has also developed a native language and cultural curriculum for schoolchildren. It faces a significant task in reviving these languages because of the century-long efforts, abandoned only within the past twenty years or so, of both missionaries and the federal government to discourage schools from teaching native languages. As a result of such discouragement, of the six thousand or so First Nations Yukoners, only about six hundred today can speak Athapaskan.

The organization rapidly turned into an influential territorial force, supported in part by churches that wanted to support the natives' search for social justice. The native position was further strengthened by the simple fact that the Yukon First Nations had never signed a treaty with the whites. This was significant because the Canadian government had long held that it remained committed to the terms of the Royal Proclamation of 1763, which required a treaty before any native lands were taken over by whites. Yet by 1962, less than 8 square miles (21 square kilometers) of the Yukon had been officially "given" to the First Nations people.

By the 1970s, the Yukon Native Brotherhood was growing more confident and more radical. In 1973, it joined together with another native organization to form the Council for Yukon Indians. The council issued a wide-ranging document that year titled "Together Today for Our Children Tomorrow." It called for the transfer of substantial tracts of land to the natives, cash payments to compensate for previous losses of

■ *A Canadian Indian poses at the fence marking the border of his reservation.*

■ First Nations a Large Minority

Starting in 1996, ethnic data was included for the first time in Canada's official census. As of 1996, approximately 12 percent of the territorial population claimed First Nations status. Additionally, another 9 percent reported that they had a partial First Nations heritage. Natives thus form a much larger percentage of the Yukon population than in any Canadian province— the overall Canadian average for First Nations status is only 1.7 percent of the population.

land, resource royalty revenues, and sweeping educational reforms. Elijah Smith, first chief of the Yukon Native Brotherhood, said, "We need a treaty to tell us what our rights are— where our land is—we want to plan for the future of our people."[26]

First Steps Toward an Agreement

Prime Minister Pierre Trudeau's Canadian government responded, perhaps recognizing the government's legal vulnerability on the treaty issue. In 1974 it created the Office of Native Claims to negotiate with Yukon Indians and other native groups. These negotiations continued back and forth for many years. It was not until May 1993 that an agreement was finally signed. The federal government, the territorial government, and the Council for Yukon Indians reached an "Umbrella Final Agreement" which the Yukon territorial legislature subsequently ratified as law.

The legislation included $242.6 million in compensation to be paid out over fifteen years; 16,000 square miles (41,400 square kilometers) of settlement land retained under aboriginal ownership; the participation of First Nations representatives on various wildlife and land commissions; and a guarantee that Yukon First Nations would receive full rental revenue from surface leases and royalties from the development of nonrenewable resources on land that the First Nations own.

Also, as part of these agreements, the First Nations were granted the power to make and enact laws with respect to their lands and citizens; to tax; to provide for municipal planning; and to manage or comanage lands and resources. As historian William R. Morrison has noted:

As Canada approaches the year 2000, its future seems to be in a state of permanent uncertainty. Nothing is certain in

■ *Former prime minister Pierre Trudeau. His government initiated a dialogue with Yukon Indians on the issue of land rights.*

the North either, except that its future will be different from its past. It may not become wealthy, or even self-sufficient—it will probably continue to consume more public funds per capita than any other jurisdiction in Canada. What is most remarkable about the North at the end of the twentieth century, however, and what gold miners, missionaries, traders, Mounted Policemen, and even the Native leaders of the past would find most astonishing, is the tremendous power and influence of the First Nations in the region. Less than fifty years ago, the northern First Nations were marginalized in their own country; yet today the North has truly become a "Northern Homeland" for First Nations.[27]

The First Nations in the Yukon clearly have a distinct view of the Yukon, one rooted in their history and tradition. That view, while different from later settlers, has been accorded both rights and dignity, and it continues to play an important part in the culture of the Yukon today. "Our heritage and legacy has been transmitted from one generation to the next, it has endured through many struggles, including those of the modern day, perhaps the most challenging of all," says the Council of Yukon First Nations. "Our culture is one that defines us as people, it provides identity and strength and our culture remains in a state of survival, a component that lives

■ *An Inuit woman cradles a child swaddled in a blanket.*

on through necessity. Our culture gives us hope and happiness, it provides vision for the future and it provides to us a profound connection to the past."[28]

First Nations of the Yukon have ultimately proved to be a resilient people, as much as the general population has been. Yukoners, both native and white, view themselves as a special breed, and given the continuing challenges they face, perhaps they are.

The Last Frontier

The Yukon has been often called the last frontier for good reason. The Yukon encompasses a truly vast land. As Canadian writer Melody Webb wrote of the region,

> Despite excursions into it by the modern world, it remains virtually untouched by permanent intrusions. It still provides a setting that nourishes the last frontier, and also one that illuminates patterns of history and environment that makes each frontier unique but that are likewise common to all. Because of the timeless quality of the Yukon, the last frontier could turn out to be an enduring frontier.[29]

Yukoners believe the real wealth of the Yukon has barely been scratched. Much of the Yukon's uniqueness lies not in the land, however, but rather in the people who rose above the challenges to stay, and who today continue to rise above economic hardships, despite the uncertainty and instability.

Throughout its history, the Yukon has tested the people who came to seek wealth and independence in its domain. First the fur trade and then the Klondike gold rush set the tenor for what was to follow. Author Pierre Berton noted that a surprising number of public figures came from a Klondike background. "The Klondike experience had taught all these men that they were capable of a kind of achievement they had never dreamed possible," he wrote.

> It was this, perhaps more than anything else, that set them apart from their fellows. In the years that followed, they tended to run their lives as if they were scaling a perpetual Chilkoot, secure in the knowledge that any obstacle, real or imagined, can be conquered by a determined man. For each had come to realize that the great stampede, with all its searchings and its yearnings, with all its bitter surprises, its thorny impediments, and its unexpected fulfillments, was, in a way, a rough approximation to life itself.[30]

Today, in its own way, the Yukon continues to foster much the same attitude. In that sense, one of the few constants in the Yukon is the people themselves. Governments, traders, missionaries, mining outfits, and construction companies may come and go. But for the First Nations people and for the relatively few others who have committed themselves to the territory, the Yukon is the only homeland they wish to have.

Facts About the Yukon Territory

Government

- Form: Parliamentary system with federal and territorial levels; Legislative Assembly consists of 17 elected members and functions in much the same way as a provincial legislature
- Highest officials: an elected premier and a federally appointed commissioner
- Federal representation: one member of parliament and one senator
- Capital: Whitehorse
- Entered confederation: June 13, 1898
- Territorial flag: green (symbolizing forest) and blue (rivers and lakes) vertical panels flank a white (snow) panel with the Yukon Coat of Arms, which features a malamute on top of a shield framed by two stems of fireweed

Land

- Area: 186,660 square miles (483,450 square kilometers); 4.8% of total land of Canada; ninth largest of provinces and territories; rivers and lakes cover approximately 0.9% of Yukon's area
- Boundaries: bordered on the south by British Columbia and Alaska, and on the west by Alaska, on the north by

the Beaufort Sea of the Arctic Ocean, and on the east by the Northwest Territories

- National parks: Kluane, Ivvavik, Vuntut
- Territorial parks: Herschel, Coal River Springs
- Highest point: Mount Logan in the St. Elias Mountains, 19,551 feet (5,959 meters); highest mountain in Canada and second-highest in North America
- Largest lake: Kluane, 118 square miles (306 square kilometers); Teslin and Tagish are larger but are partly in British Columbia
- Other major lakes: Tagish, Teslin Frances, Mayo, Laberge, Little Salmon
- Longest river: Yukon, 1,979 miles (3,185 kilometers), from source in British Columbia to mouth in Alaska (Yukon holds approximately one-third of its total length); fifth-longest river in North America
- Other major rivers: Peel, Porcupine, Ross, Liard, Snake
- Time zone: Pacific Standard Time
- Geographical extremes: 60°N to 69°N latitude; 124°W to 141°W longitude

Climate

- Coldest day: −81°F (−63°C) in Snag on Feb. 3, 1947 (lowest recorded temperature in North America)
- Warmest day: 97°F (36°C) in Mayo on June 14, 1969
- Greatest number of consecutive days with highest temperature above 90°F (32°C): 4, starting June 12, 1969 in Mayo
- Highest atmospheric pressure: 107.96 kilopascals (31.88 inches mercury) in Dawson on February 2, 1989 (Canadian record)
- Greatest temperature differential in one place: 177°F (98.3°C) in Mayo, difference between the 97°F (36°C) on June 14, 1969, and the −80°F (−62°C) on February. 3, 1947 (Canadian record for the greatest range of absolute temperatures)
- Difference between the average temperature of the warmest and coldest months for the Yukon as a whole: approximately 104°F (40°C)

People

- Population: 28,674 (2001 census); second-lowest population of provinces and territories; 0.01% of Canada's total population of 30,007,094

- Annual growth rate: –6.8% from 1996 to 2001 (twelfth-lowest among 13 provinces and territories)
- Density: 0.05 persons per square kilometer; national average: 3
- Location: Urban: 77% (Whitehorse), 23% rural (2 hamlets, 3 towns, 13 unincorporated communities, 4 villages, 8 rural communities)
- Predominant heritages: British, aboriginal, German, French
- Largest ethnic groups: Ukrainian, Dutch, Norwegian, Swedish
- Primary languages (first learned and still understood): 86% English, 9% aboriginal, 0.4% French, 4% other
- Largest (and only) city: Whitehorse, population 21,405
- Largest towns: Dawson (1,287), Watson Lake (993)
- Life expectancy at birth: 3-year average 1995–1997: Men 72.3 years; women 79.2; total both sexes 75.2, twelfth among provinces and territories (Canadian average: men 75.4; women 81.2)
- Infant mortality rate in 1996: 8.4 per 1,000 live births, eleventh among provinces and territories
- Immigration 7/1/2000–6/30/2001: 47, 0.02% of Canadian total of 252,088; second-lowest of provinces and territories
- Births 7/1/2000–6/30/2001: 360, Deaths 7/1/2000–6/30/2001: 144, Marriages in 1998: 161, Divorces in 1998: 117

Plants and animals

- Territorial bird: Raven
- Territorial flower: Fireweed
- Territorial tree: Sub-alpine fir
- Endangered, threatened, or vulnerable species: 11, including bowhead whale, Eskimo curlew, wood bison, peregrine falcon, polar bear, grizzly bear, wolverine

Holidays

- National: January 1 (New Year's Day); Good Friday; Easter; Easter Monday; Monday preceding May 25 (Victoria or Dollard Day); July 1 or, if this date falls on a Sunday, July 2 (Canada's birthday); 1st Monday of September (Labour Day); 2nd Monday of October (Thanksgiving);

November 11 (Remembrance Day); December 25 (Christmas); December 26 (Boxing Day)

- Territorial: Friday before last Sunday in February (Heritage Day); Monday nearest August 17 (Discovery Day)

Economy

- Gross domestic product per capita: $33,107 in 1999, third among provinces and territories and 97.8% compared to U.S. average[31]

- Gross territorial product: $1.1 billion at market prices in 2000, twelfth among the provinces and territories and 0.1% of gross national product

- Main industries: mining (lead, zinc, copper, gold, silver), tourism, forestry, construction, energy (hydroelectric, natural gas, thermal)

- Minor industries: transportation, fishing, furs

Notes

Introduction: The Spell of the Yukon

1. Martha Louise Black, *My Ninety Years*. Anchorage: Alaska Northwest, 1976, p. 59.

Chapter 1: Land of Challenge

2. Quoted in William R. Morrison, *True North: The Yukon and Northwest Territories*. Don Mills, Ontario: Oxford University Press Canada, 1998, p. 9.

3. H. Gordon-Cooper, *Yukoners: True Tales of the Yukon*. Vancouver: Riverrun, 1978, author's introduction.

4. Black, *My Ninety Years*, p. 31.

5. Melody Webb, *Yukon: The Last Frontier*. Vancouver: University of British Columbia Press, 1993, pp. 7–8.

6. Black, *My Ninety Years*, p. 24.

7. Robert Service, *The Spell of the Yukon*. New York: Dodd, Mead, 1916, p. 45.

8. Pierre Berton, *Klondike*. Toronto: Penguin Books Canada, 1972, p. 550.

9. Walter R. Hamilton, *The Yukon Story*. Vancouver: Mitchell Press, 1964, p. 199.

Chapter 2: The First Nations and Fur Traders

10. Quoted in Morrison, *True North*, p. 27.

11. Quoted in Morrison, *True North*, p. 17.

Chapter 3: Gold Brings Territorial Status

12. Quoted in Ken S. Coates and William R. Morrison, *Land of the Midnight Sun: A History of the Yukon*. Edmonton: Hurtig, 1988, p. 48.

13. Michael Cooper, *Klondike Fever*. New York: Houghton Mifflin, 1989, pp. 1–2.

14. Berton, *Klondike*, p. 60.

15. Quoted in Coates and Morrison, *Land of the Midnight Sun*, pp. 93–95.

16. Coates and Morrison, *Land of the Midnight Sun*, p. 52.

Chapter 4: Building a Modern Territory

17. Morrison, *True North*, p. 103.

Chapter 5: Daily Life, Arts, and Culture

18. Jack London, *The Call of the Wild*. New York: Macmillan, 1963, p. 18.

19. *YukonWeb*, "A Bank Clerk Comes to Town." www.yukonweb.com.

20. Berton, *Klondike*.

21. Mark Zuehlke, *The Yukon Fact Book*. Vancouver: White-cap Books, 1998, pp. 70–71.

Chapter 6: Unique Challenges Continue

22. Zuehlke, *The Yukon Fact Book*, pp. 137–38.

23. Zuehlke, *The Yukon Fact Book*.

24. Coates and Morrison, *Land of the Midnight Sun*, pp. 286–88.

25. Quoted in Coates and Morrison, *Land of the Midnight Sun*, pp. 287–88.

26. Quoted in Zuehlke, *The Yukon Fact Book*, p. 76.

27. Morrison, *True North*.

28. *Council of Yukon First Nations*, "Natural History." www.cyfn.ca.

29. Webb, *Yukon*, p. 309.

30. Berton, *Klondike*, p. 548.

Facts About the Yukon

31. *Demographia*, "Canada: Regional Gross Domestic Product Data: 1999." www.demographia.com.

Chronology

ca. 12,000 B.C.   First Nations peoples enter area of present-day northern Canada after crossing land bridge into North America from northern Asia.

A.D.

1741   Vitus Bering sails from Siberia and sights the coast of North America.

1825   John Franklin explores arctic coast of future Yukon Territory.

1842   Hudson's Bay Company builds Fort Frances, the first fort in the Yukon; they begin to trade with the Yukon natives.

1867   Russia sells Alaska to the United States.

1895   A small detachment of the Northwest Mounted Police arrives in the Yukon.

1896   George Carmack and two native partners, Skookum Jim Mason and Tagish Charlie, stake gold discovery claims on Rabbit Creek, setting the stage for the Klondike gold rush.

1897   The *Portland* arrives in Seattle with "a ton of gold," sparking off the Klondike gold rush.

1898   Yukon becomes a separate territory divided from the Northwest Territories; it is governed by a federally appointed commissioner and council.

1900   Completion of the White Pass and Yukon Railway, running between Skagway, Alaska, and Whitehorse, Yukon.

1919   Lead and silver mining begin at Keno Hill.

1942   American troops and American and Canadian civilians complete building the Alaska Highway.

1953   The Yukon capital is moved from Dawson City to Whitehorse.

1973   Yukon First Nations land claims negotiations begin.

1979   The 450-mile (730-kilometer) Dempster Highway, begun in 1959, is completed, running from near Dawson across the northern Yukon through the Richardson Mountains to Inuvik, Northwest Territories.

1993   Four Yukon First Nations and the governments of Canada and the Yukon Territory meet to sign the First Nation Final Land Claim and Self-Government Agreements.

1995   Judy Gingell appointed as first aboriginal commissioner.

For Further Reading

Anthony Hocking, *The Yukon and Northwest Territories*.
Toronto: McGraw-Hill Ryerson, 1979. Comprehensive yet
clearly written, with numerous photographs.

Jack London, *The Call of the Wild*. New York: Macmillan,
1963. A compelling story of the Klondike gold rush days,
from the point of view of a sled dog named Buck.

R.G. Moyles, ed., *From Duck Lake to Dawson City*. Saskatoon,
Saskatchewan: Western Producer Prairie Books, 1977.
Ebenezer McAdams' diary detailing the companionship
and hardships experienced by the men who journeyed to
the Klondike.

T.W. Paterson, *Ghost Towns of the Yukon*. Toronto: Doubleday
Canada, 1996. Paterson tells the story of the gold rush,
with special attention to describing the various camps
and forts that were set up.

Larry Pyne, *The Forgotten Trail*. Toronto: Doubleday Canada,
1996. A fascinating report on a modern-day journey following the old Stikine Trail to the Klondike.

Works Consulted

Pierre Berton, *Klondike*. Toronto: Penguin Books Canada, 1972. Written as a story, this book is a compelling read.

Martha Louise Black, *My Ninety Years*. Anchorage: Alaska Northwest, 1976. A detailed autobiography recounting life in the Yukon, beginning with the gold rush years.

Ken S. Coates and William R. Morrison, *Land of the Midnight Sun: A History of the Yukon*. Edmonton: Hurtig, 1988. A detailed account of the land and the people from the days before the fur trade until 1988.

Michael Cooper, *Klondike Fever*. New York: Houghton Mifflin, 1989. Very easy reading and packed with photographs.

H. Gordon-Cooper, *Yukoners: True Tales of the Yukon*. Vancouver: Riverrun, 1978. Short stories about men who lived through the rough-and-tumble times in the Yukon.

Walter R. Hamilton, *The Yukon Story*. Vancouver: Mitchell Press, 1964. Written in a formal manner, this book offers not only the history of the Yukon but also short stories about some of the Sourdoughs, as well as poetry.

Alan S. Kesselheim, *Going Inside: A Couple's Journey of Renewal into the North*. Toronto: McClelland and Stewart, 1995. A personal account of a couple's one-year journey through the north.

Edward McCourt, *The Yukon and Northwest Territories.* Toronto: Macmillan Canada, 1969. McCourt makes the Yukon come alive with his rich descriptions of the land and the colorful characters of the Klondike.

William R. Morrison, *True North: The Yukon and Northwest Territories.* Don Mills, Ontario: Oxford University Press Canada, 1998. A comprehensive history of Canada's northland, focusing on the Yukon.

Geoffrey Roy, *North Canada: The Bradt Travel Guide.* Guilford, CT: Globe Pequot Press, 2000. This guide is filled with suggestions for the traveler, with a small section on the Yukon.

Robert Service, *The Spell of the Yukon.* New York: Dodd, Mead, 1916. Memorable poetry about a spectacular land.

Melody Webb, *Yukon: The Last Frontier.* Vancouver: University of British Columbia Press, 1993. Very formal, university level writing with plenty of illustrations, photos, and maps.

Mark Zuehlke, *The Yukon Fact Book.* Vancouver: Whitecap Books, 1998. Everything you ever wanted to know about the territory, listed alphabetically.

Internet Sources

Council of Yukon First Nations, "Natural History." www.cyfn.ca.

Demographia, "Canada Regional Gross Domestic Product Data: 1999." www.demographia.com.

YukonWeb, "A Bank Clerk Comes to Town." www.yukonweb.com.

Index

Picture Credits

Cover Photo: ©Danny Lehman/CORBIS
AP Photo/Canadian Press, 93
©Bettmann/CORBIS, 44, 54, 55, 94
Colorado Historical Society, 40
©Corel Corporation, 10 (bottom), 14, 15, 17, 19 (both),
23, 28 (bottom), 38, 41, 77 (top), 86
Chris Jouan, 10 (top), 12, 27, 29, 67
©Clarence W. Norris/Lone Pine Photo, 33, 46, 66
©CORBIS, 20, 21, 26, 35, 45
Dover Publications, Inc., 49
©Gunter Marx Photo/CORBIS, 70, 72, 75
©Phil Hoffman/Lone Pine Photo, 59, 62, 73
Hulton Archive by Getty Images, 31, 42, 50, 84, 89, 91
Prints Old and Rare, 48, 58
Library of Congress, 28 (top), 77 (bottom), 80
PhotoDisc, 30, 63, 65
©Werner Forman/CORBIS, 32

About the Authors

Steven Ferry (www.words-images.com) writes and photographs for U.S. publishers and corporations. He has written over a dozen books, several for middle schools.

Blake Harris is a writer and journalist with more than thirty years of experience. He specializes in government, technology, and social reform issues.

Liz Szynkowski worked in education for more than twenty years before turning to professional writing and photography.

J917.19 FERRY
Ferry, Steven
Yukon Territory

$27.45

DATE			

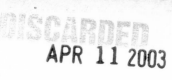

APR 11 2003

SOUTH HUNTINGTON
PUBLIC LIBRARY
2 MELVILLE ROAD
HUNTINGTON STATION, N.Y. 11746

BAKER & TAYLOR